Global Consumer Organi...

CH00555584

As corporate activity continues to expand in line with the continued globalization of the economy, there is an increasing demand for establishing rules to regulate the trans-boundary activities of firms and their many and complex relations with consumers. Until now, sources of knowledge in this field have been scattered and unsystematic, and this volume fills an important gap in current literature.

The book:

- Provides a historical overview that traces the early attempts made before the Second World War to formulate elements of global consumer policy, highlighting key issues, and initiatives up to the 1980s.
- Outlines the groups of organizations that are responsible for dealing with consumer issues in areas such as trade and development, socio-economics and the environment, including the Organisation for Economic Co-operation and Development, World Trade Organization, International Monetary Fund, United Nations Conference on Trade and Development, and World Bank.
- Analyses the group of special intergovernmental organizations that address the problems of specific consumer segments, industries, and service providers, including the World Health Organization, International Telecommunication Union and World Tourism Organization.
- Evaluates current and future challenges and dilemmas facing consumer organizations and addresses the continuing issues of coordination between them.
- Studies the role played by organizations in the consumer movement as well as the contributions of organized business and the different initiatives of self-regulation.

Providing a much needed overview of this key area in international organization, *Global Consumer Organizations* will be of interest to students and scholars in a range of areas, including international political economy, international organizations, global governance, economic policy, and consumer behaviour.

Karsten Ronit is Associate Professor of Political Science at the Department of Political Science, University of Copenhagen, Denmark.

Global Institutions

Edited by Thomas G. Weiss
The CUNY Graduate Center, New York, USA
and Rorden Wilkinson
University of Sussex, Brighton, UK

About the series

The "Global Institutions Series" provides cutting-edge books about many aspects of what we know as "global governance." It emerges from our shared frustrations with the state of available knowledge—electronic and print-wise, for research and teaching—in the area. The series is designed as a resource for those interested in exploring issues of international organization and global governance. And since the first volumes appeared in 2005, we have taken significant strides toward filling conceptual gaps.

The series consists of three related "streams" distinguished by their blue, red, and green covers. The blue volumes, comprising the majority of the books in the series, provide user-friendly and short (usually no more than 50,000 words) but authoritative guides to major global and regional organizations, as well as key issues in the global governance of security, the environment, human rights, poverty, and humanitarian action among others. The books with red covers are designed to present original research and serve as extended and more specialized treatments of issues pertinent for advancing understanding about global governance. And the volumes with green covers—the most recent departure in the series—are comprehensive and accessible accounts of the major theoretical approaches to global governance and international organization.

The books in each of the streams are written by experts in the field, ranging from the most senior and respected authors to first-rate scholars at the beginning of their careers. In combination, the three components of the series—blue, red, and green—serve as key resources for faculty, students, and practitioners alike. The works in the blue and green streams have value as core and complementary readings in courses on, among other things, international organization, global governance, international law, international relations, and international political economy; the red volumes allow further reflection and investigation in these and related areas.

The books in the series also provide a segue to the foundation volume that offers the most comprehensive textbook treatment available dealing with all the major issues, approaches, institutions, and actors in contemporary global governance—our edited work *International Organization and Global Governance* (2014)—a volume to which many of the authors in the series have contributed essays.

Understanding global governance—past, present, and future—is far from a finished journey. The books in this series nonetheless represent significant steps toward a better way of conceiving contemporary problems and issues as well as, hopefully, doing something to improve world order. We value the feedback from our readers and their role in helping shape the on-going development of the series.

A complete list of titles appears at the end of this book. The most recent titles in the series are:

World Trade Organization (2nd edition, 2015)
by Bernard M. Hoekman and Petros C. Mavroidis

Women and Girls Rising (2015)
by Ellen Chesler and Terry McGovern

The North Atlantic Treaty Organization (2nd edition, 2015)
by Julian Lindley-French

Governing Climate Change (2nd edition, 2015)
by Harriet Bulkeley and Peter Newell

The Organization of Islamic Cooperation (2015)
by Turan Kayaoglu

Contemporary Human Rights Ideas (2nd edition, 2015)
by Bertrand G. Ramcharan

The Politics of International Organizations (2015)
edited by Patrick Weller and Xu Yi-chong

Global Consumer Organizations

Karsten Ronit

Routledge
Taylor & Francis Group

LONDON AND NEW YORK

First published 2015
by Routledge
2 Park Square, Milton Park, Abingdon, Oxon OX14 4RN

and by Routledge
711 Third Avenue, New York, NY 10017

Routledge is an imprint of the Taylor & Francis Group, an informa business

British Library Cataloguing in Publication Data
A catalogue record for this book is available from the British Library

Library of Congress Cataloging in Publication Data
A catalog record for this book has been requested

ISBN: 978-0-415-67340-2 (hbk)
ISBN: 978-0-415-67341-9 (pbk)
ISBN: 978-1-315-67391-2 (ebk)

Typeset in Times New Roman
by Taylor & Francis Books

Contents

Illustrations

Figures

Tables

Boxes

Acknowledgement

This book project began many years ago, in my mind at least, when I discovered that relatively little had been written on the role of organized consumers in national and international policy-making, and that this complex policy field evolved through the contributions of many public and private actors. I further noticed that scholarly interest in organized consumers, and consumer policy more broadly, lagged far behind the interest in organized labor and environmental groups. Perhaps it was easier to develop sympathies with suppressed workers and their cause, or with environmental activists and their struggles, than with consumers who endeavor mainly to improve their position within the market economy, rather than challenge the economic system as such. While this lacuna in research and its possible backgrounds somehow lingered in my mind, it took me many years to move into studying consumer policy and its various actors more concretely; but, following the publication of two books on Danish consumer policy, I decided to analyze the work of global organizations. Although national consumer policies have their distinct features, it is increasingly difficult to separate domestic from international domains.

Over a number of years, I have reflected on this project and discussed certain aspects with colleagues during sabbaticals at McMaster University (William D. Coleman, Robert O'Brien, Tony Porter), Elliott School of International Affairs (Harvey Feigenbaum, Martha Finnemore, Susan K. Sell), Yale University (Graeme Auld, Benjamin Cashore, Connie McDermott), and the University of Washington-Seattle (Peter May, Aseem Prakash). In addition, I have had many talks on similar issues with old friends and colleagues, such as Bob Reinalda and Volker Schneider; I am grateful to all for discussions and helpful comments. Thanks also go to my colleagues at my home university, to Jørgen Dejgård Jensen for discussing different aspects of nutrition and consumer policy with me, and to Martin Marcussen for sharing his thoughts about the role of international organizations. Conversations with these people have been very helpful but, of course, none of them can be held responsible for the final result.

Along the way I have participated in other projects on international organizations, public policy, and organized business, and they have informed my research and added important perspectives to the study, although at times they have also distracted my attention and slowed down the process of writing. It was when I signed a contract with Routledge in the series Global Institutions that I found a suitable format for analyzing the role of the many different Global Consumer Organizations – embracing intergovernmental as well as non-governmental organizations – and was able to make real headway. As series editors, Rorden Wilkinson and Thomas G. Weiss have been most optimistic and encouraging throughout the process, and made many useful suggestions. I also owe thanks to the anonymous reviewers of the manuscript and to Nicola Parkin at Routledge for chasing me and seeing the project through the different stages of production.

Karsten Ronit
February 2015

Abbreviations

ACSoMP	WHO Advisory Committee on Safety of Medicinal Products
ACVFG	Air Crash Victims Families Group
AFI	Alliance for Financial Inclusion
API	Advance Passenger Information
ASC	Aquaculture Stewardship Council
B20	B20 Coalition
BARMA	Business Action for Responsible Marketing and Advertising
BCBS	Basel Committee on Banking Supervision
BIAC	Business and Industry Advisory Committee to the OECD
BIPM	International Bureau of Weights and Measures
BIS	Bank for International Settlements
CBD	Convention on Biological Diversity
CCC	Clean Clothes Campaign
CCN	Consumer Citizen Network
CCP	Committee on Consumer Policy (OECD)
CCW	Consumer Cooperatives Worldwide
CFS	Committee on World Food Security
CGAP	Consultative Group to Assist the Poor
CI	Consumers International
COPOLCO	ISO Committee on Consumer Policy
COPs	Conferences of the Parties
CSD	United Nations Commission on Sustainable Development
CSPI	Center for Science in the Public Interest
CUTS	Consumer Unity & Trust Society
DESA	United Nations Department of Economic and Social Affairs

DITC	Division on International Trade in Goods and Services, and Commodities
EC	European Community
ECOSOC	Economic and Social Council (UN)
ESC	Education for Sustainable Consumption
ESOMAR	World Association for Social, Opinion and Market Research
EU	European Union
FAO	Food and Agriculture Organization of the United Nations
FIA	Fédération Internationale de l'Automobile
FinCoNet	International Financial Consumer Protection Organisation
FLO	Fairtrade Labelling Organizations International
FSAP	Financial Sector Assessment Program
FSB	Financial Stability Board
FSC	Forest Stewardship Council
FTC	Federal Trade Commission
G20	Group of Twenty
GATT	General Agreement on Tariffs and Trade
GCET	Global Code of Ethics for Tourism
GFEI	Global Fuel Economy Initiative
GILF	Global Industry Leaders Forum
GMO	genetically modified organisms
GOTS	Global Organic Textile Standard
GPFI	Global Partnership for Financial Inclusion
GPU	General Postal Union
GRID	Global Regulators–Industry Dialogue
GSTC	Global Sustainable Tourism Council
GSTO	Global Sustainable Tourism Organization
HAI	Health Action International
HCMI	Hotel Carbon Measurement Initiative
HIS	Cluster of Health Systems and Innovation
IAA	International Advertising Association
IACC	International AntiCounterfeiting Coalition
IAC-DESD	UN Inter-Agency Committee for the Decade on Education for Sustainable Development
IACFO	International Association of Consumer Food Organizations
IAEA	International Atomic Energy Agency
IAIS	International Association of Insurance Supervisors
IAPA	International Airline Passengers Association

IAPO	International Alliance of Patients Organizations
IATA	International Aviation Transport Association
IBFAN	International Baby Food Action Network
ICA	International Co-operative Alliance
ICANN	Internet Corporation for Assigned Names and Numbers
ICAO	International Civil Aviation Organization
ICC	International Chamber of Commerce
ICIUM	International Conferences on Improving Use of Medicines
ICN	International Competition Network
ICPEN	International Consumer Protection and Enforcement Network
ICPSC	International Consumer Product Safety Caucus
ICRT	International Consumer Research & Testing
IFBA	International Food and Beverage Alliance
IFC	International Finance Corporation
IFPMA	International Federation of Pharmaceutical Manufacturers & Associations
IHR	International Health Regulations (WHO)
ILO	International Labour Organization
IMC	International Maritime Committee
IMF	International Monetary Fund
IMO	International Maritime Organization
IMPACT	International Medical Products Anti-Counterfeiting Taskforce
IMSN	International Marketing Supervision Network
INCSOC	International Network of Civil Society Organisations on Competition
INFE	OECD International Network on Financial Education
INFOSAN	International Food Safety Authorities Network
IOCU	International Organization of Consumers Unions
IOSA	IATA Operational Safety Audit
IOSCO	International Organization of Securities Commissions
IPC	Interagency Pharmaceutical Coordination group
IPCC	Intergovernmental Panel on Climate Change
IPPC	International Plant Protection Convention
ISA	International Federation of the National Standardizing Associations
ISAGO	IATA Safety Audit for Ground Operations
ISEAL	International Social and Environmental Accreditation and Labeling
ISO	International Organization for Standardization

ITA	Information Technology Agreement
ITU	International Telegraph Union
ITU	International Telecommunication Union
IWGPS	Intersecretariat Working Group on Price Statistics
KPCS	Kimberley Process Certification Scheme
MAC	Multi-stakeholder Advisory Committee
MCCA	Ministerial Council on Consumer Affairs
MNC	multinational corporation
MNE	multinational enterprise
MSC	Marine Stewardship Council
NCUC	Non-Commercial Users Constituency
NGO	non-governmental organization
OAS	Organization of American States
OECD	Organisation for Economic Co-operation and Development
OHCHR	Office of the High Commissioner for Human Rights
OICA	International Organization of Motor Vehicle Manufacturers
OIE	World Organization for Animal Health
PAN	Pesticide Action Network
PIC	Pharmaceutical Inspection Convention
PIC	Pharmaceutical Inspection Co-operation Scheme
QSM	Quality Assurance and Safety of Medicines
SARPS	Standards and Recommended Practices
SCP	Sustainable Consumption and Production
SOLAS	International Convention for the Safety of Life at Sea
SPS	Sanitary and Phytosanitary Measures
StB	Simplifying the Business
TACD	Transatlantic Consumer Dialogue
TBT	Technical Barriers to Trade
The Code	Code of Conduct for the Protection of Children from Sexual Exploitation in Travel and Tourism
TJN	Tax Justice Network
TRIPS	Trade-Related Aspects of Intellectual Property Rights
UMC	Uppsala Monitoring Centre
UN	United Nations
UN DESD	UN Decade of Education for Sustainable Development
UN Habitat	United Nations Human Settlements Programme
UN Women	United Nations Entity for Gender Equality and the Empowerment of Women
UNAIDS	Joint United Nations Programme on HIV/AIDS
UNCCD	UN Convention to Combat Desertification

UNCED	United Nations Conference on Environment and Development
UNCITRAL	United Nations Commission on International Trade Law
UNCTAD	United Nations Conference on Trade and Development
UNCTC	United Nations Centre on Transnational Corporations
UNDP	United Nations Development Programme
UNECE	United Nations Economic Commission for Europe
UNEP	United Nations Environment Programme
UNESCO	United Nations Educational, Scientific and Cultural Organization
UNFCCC	United Nations Framework Convention on Climate Change
UNFPA	United Nations Population Fund
UNGPs	United Nations Guiding Principles on Business and Human Rights
UNHCR	Office of the United Nations High Commissioner for Refugees
UNICEF	United Nations Children's Fund
UNIDO	United Nations Industrial Development Organization
UNISDR	United Nations Office for Disaster Reduction
UNITAR	United Nations Institute for Training and Research
UNODC	United Nations Office on Drugs and Crime
UNSCN	United Nations Standing Committee on Nutrition
UNU	United Nations University
UNWTO	World Tourism Organization
WBCSD	World Business Council for Sustainable Development
WCTE	World Committee on Tourism Ethics
WDC	World Diamond Council
WEF	World Economic Forum
WFA	World Federation of Advertisers
WFP	World Food Programme
WFTO	World Fair Trade Organization
WGTCP	Working Group on the Interaction between Trade and Competition Policy
WHO	World Health Organization
WIPO	World Intellectual Property Organization
WSSD	World Summit on Sustainable Development
WTAAA	World Travel Agents Associations Alliance
WTO	World Trade Organization
WTTC	World Travel & Tourism Council
WWF	World Wide Fund for Nature

Introduction

- **Defining an ill-defined field**
- **The diversity of global consumer organizations**
- **Outline of the book**

With the globalization of the economy and the expansion of corporate activity, there is an increasing demand for establishing rules to regulate the trans-boundary activities of firms and their many and complex relations with consumers. Following Polanyi's dictum that markets are embedded in many social relations and are not institution-free,[1] but need various forms of political intervention to unfold, function, adapt and reform, a variety of organizations become an object of scrutiny. Indeed, the global economy is supposed to work against a backdrop of rules enabling exchanges and the building of trust into different types of relations in the marketplace. Many of these rules are formulated, adopted and implemented in national and regional contexts, but in addition to these efforts, consumer policy has become a global concern, with activities at the level of global organizations. Although regulation does not automatically accompany and keep pace with economic globalization – a factor impeding the organization of global consumer policy – interesting developments can be observed.

There are several historical examples of consumer-related regulation in the global realm, but these precursors in various economic fields have not always been categorized as consumer regulation *per se*.[2] Globalization processes in the established capitalist economies have been significant in recent years, however, and the introduction of new market economies in the former socialist countries and the rise of the BRIC countries show that more countries and continents are becoming integrated into the world economy, epitomizing the trends towards globalization. Amid these developments, different global consumer organizations respond to new demands and address a rich diversity of issues.

Defining an ill-defined field

Consumers – and consumer policies and consumer organizations – are hard to define in general, but also when they pertain to the global scene. Consumers are attributed different names in relation to a variety of products and services, and this gives us a hint about the diversity of markets and exchanges. Apart from the universal and all-embracing "consumers," we find buyers, clients, customers, depositors, guests, passengers, patients, tenants, users, viewers, visitors, and many more that exist in different market settings. What essentially characterizes these consumer roles and functions, however, is the fact that they do not constitute a trade themselves, and unlike manufacturers and distributors,[3] which are commercial users in the production and value chain, end-consumers are always buyers, not sellers.

In economic theory, a classic observation is that the seller generally has access to more and better information than the buyer, and information asymmetries between the two parties prevail.[4] This situation is further exacerbated in the era of globalization, because consumers are less mobile than corporations and are often tied to their local context, while many corporations are engaged in trans-boundary operations and become increasingly global.[5] Different strategies are available to correct these different positions of consumers and business. Efficient and transparent markets can provide consumers with more and reliable information, but improved information is not enough, and also various legal rights are needed to protect the consumers in a variety of markets.

Mapping different segments of consumers and their concerns is a highly complex process at the global level.[6] Indeed, consumers form a vast and heterogeneous category covering the entire globe from the most affluent countries to the poorest corners of the world, and hence some consumers have access to, and purchase, a rich diversity of goods, while others are denied these opportunities. North–South cleavages are of great importance and filter into the work of global consumer organizations. In principle, these organizations need to address and encompass all continents to qualify as genuinely global,[7] but there is not always full and equal coverage, and not all kinds of consumers and markets are embraced by these efforts.

Globalization is a process rather than an end stage, and before there was a global consumer policy, or at least the building blocks of it, there were – and still are – national consumer policies.[8] These are certainly not in all countries, and are not equally mature, but national traditions and models emerged first. Gradually steps were taken to coordinate across countries and respond to common challenges, capacity was built into existing institutions, and new initiatives and bodies emerged at the global level. In the mid-1980s, an important initiative was the adoption of the United Nations Guidelines for Consumer Protection,[9] which showed that consumer policy could not be isolated to particular segments of consumers, certain products or the most affluent parts of the world, but needed to be addressed by a variety of organizations and integrated into many policy fields. Greater attention is today directed toward consumer issues, but our knowledge about global consumer organizations is still scattered and unsystematic, which in part reflects the institutional fragmentation of the area,[10] and the sidelining of consumer issues by other and more powerful economic and political agendas.

This book concentrates on the efforts to confer centrality on the consumer perspective, and we zoom in on those strategies and regulations that are adopted by global consumer organizations. It is important that we identify and analyze key principles and major initiatives because they demonstrate the areas in which the consumer perspective is particularly highlighted, and because these principles and initiatives, once established, are often employed when approaching new issues.

However, consumer issues are intertwined with other concerns, and they are hosted by different organizations in complex ways. There are many areas in which the consumer focus is less purposeful and clear, or perhaps even hidden, and consequently it must be closely searched for. In competition policy and trade policy, for instance, the betterment of consumers is not foregrounded, and here the consumer cause assumes a secondary role relative to other economic and social goals. There are also areas where it is difficult to represent the undisguised perspective of consumerism – especially if conflicting with development, environment or human rights issues. Here consumer interests must be reconciled with and integrated into other societal goals. Indeed, it is beneficial for the consumer perspective to travel with other, occasionally more dominant agendas in, for instance, food policy, health policy or technology policy, and accordingly various policy combinations are managed by global consumer organizations and must be captured in our study.

The diversity of global consumer organizations

We need to take a broad approach to understanding the elements of consumer policy and the activities of global consumer organizations. In this book, consumer organizations are not solely organizations *of* consumers, *by* consumers and *for* consumers, and the role of a variety of both intergovernmental and non-governmental organizations must be included in a modern governance perspective. Following this approach, we examine the key players involved in producing agendas, principles and rules guiding the field of global consumer politics – namely public institutions, in the form of intergovernmental agencies; civil society, by way of various consumer groups; and business, through business associations and other collective entities involved in consumer affairs. In other words, global consumer organizations refer to those major organizations that, in one way or another, focus attention on this diverse policy field. The different organizations do not necessarily cover the whole world, but they aspire to become global; they do not necessarily represent consumers, but they actively engage in issues of importance to consumers; they do not necessarily engage in consumer questions alone, but in many cases their dedication is only partial; and the organizations are not always constituted as formal and permanent bodies, but sometimes take the form of alliances and various loose forms of cooperation.

By examining the role of several types of global organizations in the shaping of consumer policy, we look for different types of influences and, consequently, debunk approaches that pay tribute to only certain actors and policies and leave others untouched. Of concern are not just the challenges facing intergovernmental organizations, not merely the responses of business associations bringing together self-interested corporations, and not only the activities of consumer groups. Indeed, all these dimensions must be included to grasp the diversity of global consumer organizations. The book gives more space to the complex world of the intergovernmental organizations, but it is important to understand that both the consumer movement and the business associations are often working inside these forums, and typically formulate their strategies in these institutional contexts, so the treatment of their role will be a part of this analysis. However, we also need to treat them separately, and here their organizations and strategies are central. Thus the different chapters in the book support each other.

Intergovernmental organizations face a special challenge to develop and reach a consensus around global policies on the basis of the various inputs of states and relevant global stakeholders. If measures must be taken to correct some of the asymmetries between business and consumers in the market, an effort can definitely be made by governments through these agencies. However, there are quite different national models and traditions to be transported onto the global realm, and also very different priorities of consumer concerns. There are also different opinions among the many private stakeholders who seek to influence the work of governments and international agencies. Aligning these different interests is not an insurmountable task, but it is a strong and enduring effort, and support from states and stakeholders is needed to make progress.

Another complicating factor is that there is no intergovernmental agency dedicated to consumer affairs alone. Unlike a number of other policy fields, there is no established and recognized institution to record past achievements, accumulate knowledge, formulate visions for the future, and in general take care of the broad and varied field of consumer affairs. Instead, we find a plethora of agencies with smaller or larger commitments: general organizations basically address issues pertaining to all consumers and all industries; special organizations attend to particular consumer segments and business sectors; and coordinating entities are tasked with bringing different organizations together in an attempt to jointly analyze a given problem and offer solutions that no single agency can provide.

Every general and special organization, in its own way, has strong expertise in relevant areas and addresses a certain group of consumer-related issues, but the lack of an encompassing consumer organization raises a number of questions relating to the possible inter-agency coordination of policy. Is it an overarching feature of consumer policy that the division of labor and specialization of agencies lead to fragmentation in global consumer policy – or do agencies somehow manage to coordinate activities through the exchange of experiences, with the purpose of formulating encompassing strategies for joint action?

Although conventional international relations studies see public policy as the clear domain of governments and intergovernmental organizations, we argue – without abandoning important research and explanations found in this tradition – that private actors formulate strategies and, in some cases, produce policies that gain authority, in much the same way as traditional public regulation does.[11]

Consumer groups are dedicated to representing the global concerns of consumers. Although these groups can be a dynamic force, they tend to be seen as atomized, fragmented, and inactive, having mainly a campaigning ability. This perception goes hand-in-hand with the view that consumers are not able to organize properly in a collective format, and hence cannot exploit their full potential as a large and diffuse group. There are different global consumer organizations, and this view ignores the fact that consumers are organized in a collective format, most encompassingly through Consumers International (CI) dating back to 1960.[12]

A further variety of consumer organizations advance consumers' interests, and also a wider group of specialized civil society organizations are very adept at identifying new issues which are not typically associated with consumer agendas. Many of these organizations do not span the same classical issues as, for instance, the CI, but they are highly competent within their own domains. Consequently, consumer organizations may effectively coordinate interests and build alliances of advocacy with other civil society groups that embrace certain aspects of consumer affairs without being consumer organizations *sensu strictu*.

Different forms of consumer participation are relevant here to help intergovernmental agencies enact regulation to protect consumers. Participation in relevant policy-making forums is usually desirable and a hallmark of official recognition, but some groups prefer to protest rather than participate. Currently, however, we also are witnessing a high degree of institutional innovation beyond the framework of international agencies. Consumer organizations can play a vital role in effectively bringing their experiences into deliberation with other private players in consumer policy, and through engagement in such processes – sometimes involving business – organized consumers endorse various initiatives.

It is evident that today, different forms of involvement are relevant from the perspective of global consumer groups. Therefore, do global consumer organizations, individually or through concerted action, take an active part in the making of traditional public policy through intergovernmental organizations, or do they engage in new and alternative forms of policy-making with other actors to shape relevant rules and norms to the benefit of consumers?

In our approach to global consumer organizations, we finally attribute an important role to the global business community. Many bodies are engaged in consumer policy, typically by way of numerous and highly diversified industry associations, or through a handful of trans-industry associations representing very large sections of business, such as the International Chamber of Commerce (ICC).

When business shows a strong interest in consumer affairs, it is because business needs rules, predictability and stability in dealing with consumers, and because consumer relations is a key factor in competition. This fact does not imply that corporations and industries will take a lead role in bringing forward concrete plans, and large parts of business will often oppose, or only hesitantly accept, regulation. Indeed, rivalries in and across industries persist between different groups of corporations.

Business action may be directed at establishing – or evading – public regulation adopted within the framework of intergovernmental organizations. However, business may have a preference for authorizing its own rules. Single-firm practices and codes can have great value in safeguarding consumers and establishing acceptable standards worldwide. These smaller schemes, however, rarely have the same character as public regulation, because they do not gain wider currency and, obviously, they are not observed by all firms in a given industry.

Private rules are extremely varied and are adopted in many contexts. This institutional diversity suggests that private rules are much harder to keep track of, although certain large schemes generating ethical behavior among corporations, such as the stewardship councils or the fair trade programs, now exist, and also include other parties beyond the business community.

Business takes a key interest in consumer affairs, and there are several avenues of organized business involvement in the shaping of consumer policy and different regulatory options. Therefore, does business prefer to have principles and rules adopted within the framework of intergovernmental agencies, or does business favor privately authorized rules, either at the level of particular industries or through broader business associations?

Outline of the book

Chapter 1 traces the few and early attempts made before the Second World War to formulate elements of global consumer policy, then highlights key issues and initiatives in the decades up to the 1980s. Over such a long time the consumer cause has experienced both ups and downs. National and regional approaches have been important, but the institutionalization of global consumer affairs is not reducible to the preferences of states, and a number of interesting initiatives have been developed in the context of intergovernmental organizations. At the same time, consumer groups have found new ways of cooperating globally: they participate in different forums, and address new challenges in relation to a variety of goods and services. Early on, business was also an active player in consumer policy, and in some cases business has contributed important solutions. The chapter emphasizes that although achievements have been made, the global policy field is difficult for different public and private bodies to organize.

The group of general organizations that deals with general consumer issues is the focus of Chapter 2. In these contexts, broader ideas, principles and regulations are discussed and adopted without being closely related to any particular commodity, industry group or segment of consumers. Although several of the organizations link up with multiple policy fields, we can try to group them. Beyond the United Nations (UN) and its Economic and Social Council (ECOSOC) as socio-economic organizations, these bodies include the Organisation for

Economic Co-operation and Development (OECD), World Bank, and International Monetary Fund (IMF); as trade and development organizations, we find the World Trade Organization (WTO), International Organization for Standardization (ISO), United Nations Conference on Trade and Development (UNCTAD), International Consumer Protection and Enforcement Network (ICPEN) and World Intellectual Property Organization (WIPO); and among the environmental organizations, the United Nations Environment Programme (UNEP) is especially relevant.

In some cases, special subunits are established by these organizations to address relevant aspects of consumer policy. Consumer policy is not the traditional stronghold of these units, but many social and economic issues have a clear bearing on consumers, as shown, for instance, by the OECD Guidelines for Multinational Enterprises. In other words, consumer policy must struggle for recognition among other and more established policies such as competition policy, economic policy, trade policy, social policy, environmental policy and development policy.

Consumer policy is not limited to agencies with such horizontal approaches. Chapter 3 studies the group of special intergovernmental organizations that addresses the problems of specific consumer segments, industries and service providers. To different degrees, these agencies draw on general principles and ideas fostered by the encompassing organizations, but they also devise their own strategies. This group of agencies includes the World Health Organization (WHO), Food and Agriculture Organization of the United Nations (FAO), International Civil Aviation Organization (ICAO), International Telecommunication Union (ITU) and World Tourism Organization (UNWTO). In these contexts, consumers are framed in different ways, illustrating the rich diversity of rules and institutional settings in which consumer issues are dealt with globally. As with the horizontal organizations, the special organizations do not have consumer policy as their primary area of policy-making, but these special organizations can nevertheless be very important.

In Chapter 4, major areas of coordination are analyzed. Many issues are managed by individual organizations without much consultation with other bodies, whereas other problems require systematic coordination. Sometimes there is no obvious agency to direct coordination, while other times there is a lead organization with a key competence, as for instance the Codex Alimentarius Commission, which is involved in nutrition issues and standard setting, and is run jointly by FAO and WHO.

The institutionalization of coordination draws on complementary resources, but coordination is occasionally related to various "turf wars," in which there are disagreements between different institutions, ideas, principles and interests. Conflicts between consumer policy and trade policy illustrate this problem, and in areas of coordination the consumer perspective does not always prevail, having only weak institutional backing.

A major argument of Chapter 5 is that the role of non-governmental organizations must be integrated into a study on global consumer organizations, and while certain aspects of their activities are discussed in the preceding chapters where the emphasis is on the complex role of the many intergovernmental organizations that ultimately can adopt rules to govern markets, this chapter focuses on the consumer and the business side. These private organizations have different interests and strategies. On the consumer side, fragmentation is strong and many smaller outfits exist, but interest representation is also centralized through CI. On the business side, there are many organizations representing different industries and products, but some organizations, such as the ICC, have a coordinating role. Not only consumer groups and business associations leverage intergovernmental organizations; private organizations also provide alternative private governance, often in areas where public regulation is weak and underdeveloped. These organizations formulate and implement rules, either alone or through multi-stakeholder arrangements that integrate different concerns.

Chapter 6 finally brings together the different findings and evaluates the work performed by the many consumer organizations, discusses the various dilemmas they face, and highlights the paths they have taken in the development and institutionalization of this complex policy field.

Notes

1 Karl Polanyi, *The Great Transformation: The Political and Economic Origins of Our Time* (New York: Farrar & Rinehart, 1944). Today this view is followed not only in economic history but also, for instance, in the branches of neo-institutional economics, socio-economics and international political economy. For some systematic attempts to categorize different public and private institutions see, for example, John Braithwaite and Peter Drahos, *Global Business Regulation* (Cambridge: Cambridge University Press, 2000); Avner Greif, "Commitment, coercion, and markets: the nature and dynamics of institutions supporting exchange," in *Handbook of New Institutional Economics*, eds C. Ménard and M. Shirley (Heidelberg: Springer, 2005), 727–86.

2 Craig N. Murphy, *International Organization and Industrial Change: Global Governance since 1850* (Cambridge: Polity Press, 1994); Bob Reinalda, *Routledge History of International Organizations: From 1815 to the Present Day* (London: Routledge, 2009).

3 National legislation differs as to how consumers are defined, but in general the same principles apply. The UN Guidelines for Consumer Protection refer, for instance, to the business side as "those responsible for bringing goods to the market" (A12), "manufacturers (producers) and distributors" (1C, A13, A14, A16, A25), "the seller" (A18, A21), "manufacturers and retailers" (A 20). UN, *The UN Guidelines for Consumer Protection* (as expanded in 1999) (New York: United Nations, 2003).

4 For classic contributions discussing the problem of information asymmetry see George Stigler, "The economics of information," *Journal of Political Economy* 69, no. 3 (1961): 213–25; Kenneth J. Arrow, "Uncertainty and the welfare economics of medical care," *American Economic Review* 53, no. 5 (1963): 941–73; George A. Akerlof, "The market for 'lemons': quality uncertainty and the market mechanism," *Quarterly Journal of Economics* 84, no. 3 (1970): 488–500.

5 The discrepancy between the fast forces of the market and the slow forces of public policy is, for instance, dealt with in studies on global public policy, see Wolfgang Reinicke, *Global Public Policy: Governing without Government?* (Washington, DC: Brookings Institution Press, 1998); William D. Coleman and Anthony Perl, "Internationalized policy environments and policy network analysis political studies," *Political Studies* 47, no. 4 (1999): 691–709; Karsten Ronit, ed., *Global Public Policy. Business and the Countervailing Powers of Civil Society* (London: Routledge, 1997); Mathias Koenig-Archibugi, "Understanding the global dimensions of policy," *Global Policy* 1, no. 1 (2010): 16–28; Diane Stone, *Knowledge Actors and Transnational Governance: The Private–Public Policy Nexus in the Global Agora* (Houndmills: Palgrave, 2013).

6 From the perspective of complexity theory different features constitute a complex field, but basically many types of actors interact at different levels around multiple and shifting issues, with the selection of strategies becoming increasingly demanding. Robert Axelrod and Michael D. Cohen, *Harnessing Complexity: Organizational Implications of a Scientific Frontier* (New York: The Free Press, 2000); Volker Schneider, "Governance and complexity," in *The Oxford Handbook of Governance*, ed. David Levi-Faur (Oxford: Oxford University Press, 2012), 129–42.

7 In consumer protection, national efforts are needed to meet the challenges of globalization, and not only in countries with weak domestic business and weak institutions. Cary Coglianese, Adam Finkel and David Zaring, eds, *Import Safety: Regulatory Governance in the Global Economy* (Philadelphia: University of Pennsylvania Press, 2009).

8 Stephen Brobeck and Robert N. Mayer, eds, *Consumer Activism: An Encyclopedia of Watchdogs and Whistleblowers* (Santa Barbara, CA: ABC-CLIO, 2015).

9 UN, *United Nations Guidelines for Consumer Protection*, A/RES/39/248, 16 April 1985 (New York: United Nations 1985), www.un.org/esa/sustdev/p ublications/consumption_en.pdf.

10 Michele Micheletti, Andreas Follesdal and Dietlind Stolle, eds, *Politics, Products, and Markets: Exploring Political Consumerism* (New Brunswick, N.J.: Transaction Publishers, 2003); Matthew Hilton, *Prosperity for All: Consumer Activism in an Era of Globalization* (Ithaca, NY and London: Cornell University Press, 2009).

11 Since the late 1990s, a growing body of literature summarizes – under both competing and complementary concepts – the role of private actors in international rule-making. For some overviews see, for instance, Claire A. Cutler, Virginia Haufler and Tony Porter, eds, *Private Authority and International Affairs* (New York: State University of New York Press, 1999); David Vogel, "Private global business regulation," *Annual Review of Political Science* 11 (2007): 261–82; Thomas Hale and David Held, eds, *The Handbook of Transnational Governance: Institutions and Innovations* (Cambridge: Polity Press, 2011).

12 Consumers International (CI) was founded as International Organization of Consumers Unions (IOCU). Consumers International, *1960–2010. 50 Years of the Global Consumer Movement* (London: Consumers International, 2010). It has members (national associations) from around 120 countries. Little research has been done on this organization, as discussed in Chapter 5.

1   Historical trajectories

- **Scattered pre-war efforts**
- **The 1940s and 1950s: free market and democracy**
- **The 1960s and 1970s: organizing consumers and their rights**
- **The 1980s and beyond: new forays and limits**
- **Conclusion**

The formation of consumer policy at the global level is strongly associated with the globalization of economies. Early forms of globalization, dating back to the beginning of the twentieth century and the interwar years, gave some important impulses, but these were still too weak to enable a proper global consumer agenda to mature, and dedicated consumer organizations in the public and private world to emerge. Indeed, economic globalization did not lead straightforwardly to the formation of consumer policies to regulate markets, and nobody had a mission, ambition or capacity to take the lead and bring greater coherence and continuity into the organization of consumer policy.

The first historical examples that we discuss, and which ultimately paved the way for later and more targeted initiatives, were rarely phrased as consumer policy, and few if any organizations understood themselves as global consumer organizations. Many events, initiatives and ideas were only sporadically associated with consumer agendas. Only much later, and with the advantage of hindsight, is it possible to see that some initiatives had a bearing on the role of global consumer organizations in later decades. In fact, these inputs came from different directions and from different types of actors, also an important feature of current global consumer policy. Thus the historical trajectories are characterized by the formation of new organizations, pioneering initiatives, and changing relations between actors who offer different approaches to help and shape different areas of consumer policy. This chapter elucidates some of these major features and offers signposts for the next chapters, in which some of the organizations and initiatives are dealt with more thoroughly.

Scattered pre-war efforts

The regulation of exchanges between producers and retailers on one hand, and consumers on the other, goes back over a long period and builds on different national traditions. A major emphasis was on the issue of competition. Given the lack of strong international efforts in the early days of economic globalization, some domestic initiatives could spill over into the global realm and serve as an inspiration. With the rise of powerful corporations leading to cartel- and trust-building before the First World War, many governments saw an imminent need to halt this development and reinstall competition. In the USA in 1914, President Wilson made a pioneering effort to set up the Federal Trade Commission (FTC) to curtail anti-competitive practices in business and to challenge the power of giant economic groups.[1] Further efforts were made in the following decades to create a competitive marketplace to the benefit of business and consumers, and this battle around competition became an international one, influencing agendas and regulation.

Competition was an issue not only within countries, but to a high degree also between countries, with international trade as one of the remedies used to overcome monopolies and to offer products at affordable prices to the consumers. Consequently, consumer issues were framed in terms of competition policy and in terms of trade policy. In this optic, free trade was important to consumers, but trade was also a key instrument to overcome protectionism in a time of crisis and foster peaceful collaboration among nations between the wars.

Competition and trade issues, and their many and complex interfaces, were dealt with at the global level by the nascent bureaucracies of some of the specialized intergovernmental bodies established in the late nineteenth and the early twentieth centuries to enable communication, enhance technical cooperation, adopt general standards and lower trade barriers. These intergovernmental bodies include the International Telegraph Union (ITU), 1865; General Postal Union (GPU, later Universal Postal Union), 1874; International Bureau of Weights and Measures (BIPM), 1875; and the International Federation of the National Standardizing Associations (ISA), 1926.[2] Issues such as intellectual property rights and patents were addressed in other forums and through other pieces of regulation. Although consumer concerns were not explicated, regulations adopted in these organizations invariably had some side effects on consumers. The same applies to organizations and regulations in the area of transport; but safety matters received special attention, and the adoption in 1914 of the International Convention for the Safety of Life at Sea (SOLAS) is a prominent example.[3]

Alongside the efforts of various special agencies, different entities under the League of Nations addressed a number of economic issues through various international conferences, where trade issues were central, and the Convention for the Abolition of Import and Export Restrictions was adopted in 1927, in a time of prosperity.[4] In addition, the League's economic and financial organization, its communication and transit organization, and its health organization also worked in areas pertaining to consumers. A number of agreements were concluded by the League, many of which had a consumer aspect.[5]

To different degrees, it was possible for non-governmental organizations to exchange with intergovernmental bodies, including the League of Nations, to influence their strategies,[6] but while business associations – in specific industries and in the business community as such – were available to represent business interests, the same capabilities were not developed on the consumer side. National consumer organizations were only in the development stage and had different philosophies. Should solutions for the betterment of consumers be found in existing society, or was a new social order desired, in which, for instance, cooperatives or socialism might be the answer?[7] And if the labor movement already represented consumers, why create specific organizations for consumers? Such factors hampered the development of consumer organization and also complicated the formation of international platforms.

While business was far better organized to exchange with relevant intergovernmental bodies, business associations also had a capacity to develop rules addressing the relations between firms and consumers. The paradigm case was delivered by the Paris-based International Chamber of Commerce (ICC), established in 1919 as a trans-industry association acting on behalf of large sections of business, but following traditions of earlier international business associability. It was engaged in a wide scope of activities and was also prolific in consumer affairs.[8] With members from around the world, it based its strategies on a profound knowledge, which was hardly available in the public system, and adopted and implemented its own rules.

An important piece of regulation was introduced in the area of advertising when, in 1937, the ICC Code on Advertising was adopted, an issue of significance for business and consumers alike.[9] The code, in a revised version, is still in force today. This piece of private regulation demonstrated, together with other initiatives, that the ICC put great emphasis on codes as a tool to regulate competition between firms as well as to shape relations between business and consumers within a stable legal framework. By developing codes, the organization took control of some areas of regulation and did not surrender authority to public agencies. Self-regulation was a viable instrument in global consumer policy, and this activity expanded over the next decades.

The 1940s and 1950s: free market and democracy

A whole new international system of organizations dawned after the Second World War, when the UN and many special agencies came into being. These formative years in the creation or re-creation of inter-governmental cooperation were critical, and influenced which policy fields needed international organizations, how labor was to be divided between them, and which areas were not sufficiently ripe for being hosted by organizations and could be accommodated in other ways. This pattern had long-lasting effects.

In this process, important bodies emerged within as well as beyond the formal UN framework and began to organize specific policy fields. To some degree, the creation of the Economic and Social Council (ECOSOC) can be seen as a continuation of some of the bodies of the League of Nations that were involved in economic affairs, and this general body became a forum for discussing consumer policy at a later stage. Also, a number of special and independent bodies emerged. A new pattern of intergovernmental cooperation was created, in which specialized policies could be formulated and regulation adopted. This potential to address consumer concerns was not immediately exploited, but some new bodies attended to different consumer issues, for instance in relation to food (Food and Agriculture Organization of the United Nations, FAO), health (World Health Organization, WHO), and air transport (International Civil Aviation Organization, ICAO).[10]

No organization, however, was mandated the job of developing consumer policy as a new field, closely related to the globalization of the economies, but the activities of different agencies spilled over into and had a bearing on consumer affairs. Important bodies were formed to address major challenges of national economies and their linkages, and were tasked with different aspects of their financial situation and economic growth. As such, they set important agendas and influenced economic thinking in a broad sense. The two Washington-based institutions, the International Monetary Fund (IMF) and the World Bank, were created according to the Bretton Woods Agreement in 1944 to re-energize the world economy after the war, and, in the long run, to create stable institutions to underpin the capitalist system in a new era. These institutions would not come to cover the entire world, and especially not embrace countries behind the "Iron Curtain," but the basic ideas promulgated by these organizations should demonstrate the superiority of market-based economies.

As part of their broad commitment, they emphasized the role of the private sector, free competition as an intrinsic value to consumers, and free trade as a crucial element in economic development and financial stability – goals not easily achieved. There was no attempt to hammer out a consumer policy to enable effective markets, and international competition and trade were assumed to do the trick and benefit consumers. In many ways the General Agreement on Tariffs and Trade (GATT), followed by the World Trade Organization (WTO) in 1995, worked along similar lines within its domain, where general policies were formulated and rules implemented with regard to specific commodities, but in the founding document, The General Agreement on Tariffs and Trade, some of the discussion was about consumers, although the general departure was from trade and competition policy.[11]

Concurrently with the rise of new organizations, new principles for their work were formulated and new practices had to be developed.[12] Alongside the cooperation between states, different forms of cooperation between international agencies and private interests also developed. The principles guiding these relations were not written into the covenant of the League of Nations, but after the Second World War the UN Charter provided for such arrangements.[13] In this way, a legal framework was created to legitimize the participation of various private organizations, among which business was already far better organized at the global level through numerous associations.[14] The preference in the UN system was decidedly for granting consultative status to large and global associations. One of the first organizations to seek participatory rights was the International Co-Operative Alliance (ICA),[15] established in 1895, which represented certain segments of consumers.

From a further perspective, the principles became an important institutional innovation and an encouragement for interest groups to seek consultancy status, and for those interests not already organized in an international format to establish and coordinate through new international organizations. Although this true institutional innovation did not instantaneously open up a broad avenue of consumer participation, the new principles encouraged general national consumer organizations, which already existed or which were formed in the 1940s and 1950s, to seek closer coordination at the global level.

The 1960s and 1970s: organizing consumers and their rights

Some important conditions were created for the formation and participation of the global consumer movement in the 1940s and 1950s, but consumer groups had to establish themselves more solidly at domestic levels, and from this position reach out to global cooperation. While different national consumer organizations were founded before the Second World War, the process gained momentum in the following decades. With economic growth, the purchasing power of consumers in the industrialized countries increased, consumers had access to a rich variety of consumer goods, and stronger demands were voiced for better information and for more rights.

Of great symbolic value – but also of practical significance – was President Kennedy's Special Message to the Congress on Protecting the Consumer Interest in March 1962, in which the importance, yet weakness, of consumers was recognized:

> Consumers, by definition, include us all. They are the largest economic group in the economy, affecting and affected by almost every public and private economic decision. Two-thirds of all spending in the economy is by consumers. But they are the only important group in the economy who are not effectively organized, whose views are often not heard.[16]

The American society was the first to become what is vaguely described as a "consumer society," and considering the special economic and political weight of the USA, this message was an important signal for consumers worldwide. It became a tool for consumer organizations which did not see business and the promises of the market as automatically providing consumer access to better information and rights, or for that matter, governments as always correcting the failures of the market. Instead, an active and autonomous consumer movement was essential to halt the excessive power of business and bring about change. In addition to the material side of modern welfare society, the organization and representation of consumers could, in some industrialized countries, also be seen as forming part of a consumer model and more generally a state-building project, although there is huge variation in ideas and practices.[17] This development was very different from the situation in the developing countries, which lacked such institutions, but with the independence of an increasing number of states in the 1950s and 1960s in Africa and Asia, new consumer organizations could form part of a burgeoning civil society and enrol in global organizations. This was a development not to be accomplished overnight, but there was a strong globalizing potential for including national associations from across the continents and building representative global consumer organizations.

A breakthrough in the organization of global consumer interests came in 1960 with the foundation of the International Organization of Consumers Unions (IOCU).[18] Representing a highly diverse group of consumers, the IOCU was built as a federation with national consumer associations as members – not individual consumers – and it had a strong ambition to cover all parts of the world, as this would demonstrate a high degree of representativeness and secure greater recognition. In the early days, there was clearly a membership bias toward the affluent countries, but membership was gradually extended. However, large-scale collective action of the community of global consumers was – and still is – very demanding.

Pre-dating – and also following – the emergence of a global consumer organization, attention to consumers seeped into a range of political contexts, but as in the past many consumer issues were dealt with in fragmented ways by various special agencies and not yet, at least, much addressed by a general organization like the IOCU. However, some broader economic and social issues pertaining to all markets and to all consumers required a coordinated global response. Again, a general issue relating to competition was high on the global consumer agenda in the 1960s and 1970s, namely the role of multinational corporations (MNCs) in the global economy. This was an issue of concern to consumers, both in the wealthiest and in the poorest countries. The proliferation of MNCs could impede competition and dominate markets, this being one of the perils associated with free trade. The efforts of single governments to tame such trans-boundary actors proved insufficient, and therefore many attempts were made to advance the regulation of their activities.[19]

The role of MNCs was approached in various organizational contexts. In the UN and its ECOSOC, a study group was established, and a report with the broad title Multinational Corporations and World Development in which certain impacts of MNC activity on the conditions of consumers were addressed, was presented in 1973.[20] As a result of this report and the following deliberations, the permanent Commission on Transnational Corporations and the United Nations

Centre on Transnational Corporations (UNCTC) were established in 1974 to monitor and analyze developments. This work helped set important agendas, but it did not lead to new and stricter regulation of MNCs.

Similar developments characterized the work of the Organisation for Economic Co-operation and Development (OECD), which gradually became engaged in consumer policy and adopted various strategies and rules. As part of the Declaration on International Investment and Multinational Enterprises, the OECD Guidelines for Multinational Enterprises were adopted in 1976.[21] Originally the guidelines, which are voluntary, addressed the consumer dimension primarily through the language of competition policy, and it took some further time before explicit recommendations with respect to consumer interests were incorporated into the revised and expanded versions from the 1980s.

A number of economic and social issues were not addressed as consumer issues proper, but were framed primarily as development issues, and here the UN and United Nations Conference on Trade and Development (UNCTAD) was an important forum for policy-making. Thus the quest for a new international economic world order, put forward by developing countries through UNCTAD, highlighted the need for a set of economic relations that would be of greater benefit to this group of countries. In 1974, this campaign led to the UN Declaration on the Establishment of a New International Economic Order, which foresaw the elimination of inequalities in the economic world. Such a new order was intended to help not only the countries of the Global South, but also its consumers.[22] Like the trade-policy approaches marshalled by trade organizations promoting free trade, these broader initiatives explicitly linked trade and consumer policy, but now in a quite different version. This strategy was also expressed in the Charter of Economic Rights and Duties of States, prepared under the auspices of UNCTAD, which underlined that trade agreements should be concluded "in a manner which is remunerative for producers and equitable for producers and consumers."[23] Furthermore, and with a view to controlling business, the Set of Multilaterally Agreed Equitable Principles and Rules for the Control of Restrictive Business Practices was approved in a resolution by the United Nations Conference on Restrictive Business Practices in 1980. In this resolution, a major objective was "to protect and promote social welfare in general and, in particular, the interests of consumers in both developed and developing countries."[24] These non-binding rules have since been reviewed on various occasions.

The 1980s and beyond: new forays and limits

Many developments in the 1960s and 1970s spilled over into the 1980s and beyond. They showed that consumer policy was not just a good-weather phenomenon entirely associated with economic growth, giving concessions to consumers only when they could be afforded. Accomplishments could also be made when economies experienced a downswing. Strong forces, but not always strong enough, were launched to give the consumer cause greater priority and to organize consumer policy in the 1980s. As in preceding decades, many consumer issues were still dealt with in rather specialized forums and by a diversity of intergovernmental organizations, but in addition, efforts were made to formulate general strategies.

A major step was taken to improve the rights of consumers when, in 1985, the UN adopted The United Nations Guidelines for Consumer Protection. Formally, this document had been prepared since 1981 through ECOSOC, in a process influenced by the consumer movement led by IOCU, but the initiative must be seen in a longer perspective. It was, in many ways, a logical result of the debates and initiatives intended to address consumer issues at the UN, and to link consumer issues with development and take "into account the interests and needs of consumers in all countries, particularly those in developing countries" – as the opening section of the resolution read.[25]

While consumer issues were occasionally filtered into other resolutions that were concerned primarily with competition, trade or development, the elaborated guidelines departed from a strict consumer perspective and viewed consumer issues not in the light of other concerns, but as the primary objective to be accomplished. Their endorsement by the UN General Assembly gave the guidelines a strong authority, and their general character made them applicable to different markets and consumer segments (see Box 1.1).[26]

Box 1.1 Objectives in consumer protection

- To assist countries in achieving or maintaining adequate protection for their population as consumers.
- To facilitate production and distribution patterns responsive to the needs and desires of consumers.
- To encourage high levels of ethical conduct for those engaged in the production and distribution of goods and services to consumers.

- To assist countries in curbing abusive business practices by all enterprises at the national and international levels which adversely affect consumers.
- To facilitate the development of independent consumer groups.
- To further international cooperation in the field of consumer protection.
- To encourage the development of market conditions which provide consumers with greater choice at lower prices.
- To promote sustainable consumption.

UN, United Nations Guidelines for Consumer Protection (as expanded in 1999) (New York: United Nations, 2003).

Although the guidelines were unanimously approved, an important goal unto itself in such a forum, there were various disagreements, and the document was therefore not hailed as the Magna Carta of consumers or as a decisive breakthrough, but as an acceptable compromise. Many voices in and beyond the consumer movement felt that stricter rules should be adopted to control business, not least with regard to the operations of transnational corporations, which were discussed in many other institutional contexts. This was quite a sensitive problem, and many Western countries, especially the USA, struggled against formulations that would aim at stricter regulation of this group of corporations. Sharp resistance also came from the corporate world, including business associations such as the ICC. It was felt that too radical guidelines would turn the tables on business and give the consumer movement some powerful tools. As with many other consumer-related principles adopted in the past, however, the guidelines had a non-binding character and were issued as recommendations to assist in the further formulation of a global consumer policy and to encourage governments to implement stricter rules to advance consumer rights.

As discussed, a central goal was to advance the consumer cause in the developing countries, which often lacked institutions to guarantee the rights of consumers. Regulation was already in place in many industrialized countries, however, and experiences from these pioneering countries helped formulate the global guidelines and became an inspiration for global activities and for the implementation of regulation in countries with little consumer regulation. However, it would be an error to see the guidelines, or other initiatives for that matter, as the accumulated result of small additive changes at domestic level; many and sometimes contradictory inputs were delivered from countries with a tradition of consumer regulation, and the global process demanded new and coordinated strategies

It became a particular challenge to globalize consumer policy in the 1980s and 1990s, but the level of consumer protection differed significantly, with strong regional variations. One important development in these decades was the demise of "socialism" in the former Soviet Union, Eastern Europe, China, and a number of other countries with similar economic and political systems. Socialist models, envisaged to resolve economic and social problems between producers and consumers, were abandoned, and gradually these countries became integrated into the world economy. However, these countries, with no real consumer movement and no strong consumer regulation, could do little actively to help formulate global strategies.[27] It was a huge challenge to embrace this group of countries, raise the level of consumer protection, and educate domestic organizations to implement global principles expressed in the UN Guidelines for Consumer Protection and in rules adopted by various special agencies. Such challenges already existed in relation to many developing countries, but new complexities were added with the inclusion of former socialist countries in the world economy.

While it took time to integrate some regions into the development of global strategies, other regions advanced their consumer strategies quickly. Starting in the 1970s, the European Community (EC) (from 1993 the European Union, EU) intensified its engagement in consumer policy. New political and administrative entities were created, consumer rights were hammered out in specific sectors and industries, and a greater role was attributed to the participation of civil society.[28] These experiences enabled stronger inputs into global organizations involved in consumer affairs.

An inherent feature of globalization is the inputs delivered from global civil society as a potential contributor to global governance. Greater efforts were made to create institutions of global governance within many policy fields, including consumer policy, and in the early 1990s changes in the global political architecture were recommended by the Commission on Global Governance.[29] Institutional changes took place in many intergovernmental organizations, and thus followed in the trail laid out in the early days of the UN when a greater role was attributed to non-governmental organizations. Although some progress was made, opportunity for substantial consumer participation was not provided in, for instance, the WTO or in various global financial institutions.[30]

While economic operations have become increasingly trans-boundary, in many cases regulation has remained within boundaries, and debates on these regulatory deficits have found their way into many inter-governmental organizations. New public regulation was relevant, but also regulation provided by business became an important issue in global governance. With an ambition to harness the resources of business, in 1999 the UN Secretary-General launched what was originally called the Global Compact for the New Century (later just the UN Global Compact), an initiative backed by a number of multinational corporations. This is a voluntary arrangement, much in line with previous efforts in consumer policy where plans to impose stricter rules on business often ended in watered-down recommendations.

In the UN Global Compact, large corporations are to meet certain requirements, and are thus recognized as having some governance functions; but as discussed later in this book there has been much controversy over the appropriateness of creating such institutions and surrendering authority to business. According to this critique, private governance was not part of a genuine democratic process, and voluntary standards were too low and therefore not a proper alternative to traditional public regulation. However, it is undeniable that the role of business as a potential contributor to global consumer policy became, and still is, an important issue.

Conclusion

It took a long time for global consumer organizations to emerge and for consumer policies to materialize. For many years, consumer issues were marginally dealt with at the global level, and primarily under the auspices of intergovernmental organizations dominated by competition and trade agendas. Only occasionally were consumer concerns explicitly mentioned in the elaboration of these other policies. After the Second World War, however, consumer issues were better attended to in some forums (for instance FAO, ISO and WHO), and institutional opportunities for consumer participation were created. A major breakthrough in the empowerment of consumers came with the formation of the IOCU as an encompassing global organization dedicated to representing all consumers in the world and in all fields. As such, the organization could both advance general principles and engage in issues of concern to specific segments of consumers, but from the outset it was an enormous task to bridge divides in such a diverse constituency, especially in view of the great economic disparities in the world.

Associated with economic growth, increasing globalization of markets and diversification of consumer goods, several global organizations independently came to address the global situation of consumers, but not always in a manifest way. However, this compartmentalization was just one feature in the evolution of consumer policy. In addition, general principles were agreed to by the UN, epitomized by the UN Guidelines for Consumer Protection, which could assist the development of consumer policy in different sectors. These guidelines were useful in setting a broad agenda and encouraging further efforts at global and domestic levels, but as with a number of other general initiatives (for instance in UNCTAD and OECD), these rules had a non-binding character and displayed some of the weaknesses of global consumer regulation.

Business resistance to stricter rules was pronounced – a thread running through the history of global consumer policy. Business was able to influence policy-making in many forums; and to eschew public regulation, business sometimes took an active role and defined and administered its own solutions. There is a tradition in the global business community to develop and police rules, and some coordination was achieved, for instance through the ICC as a leading global business association. Many private initiatives, however, did not follow a general line, and were fostered by individual industries and producer groups and adapted to their specific conditions. Much fragmentation therefore prevailed in the initiatives of business.

Notes

1 For the general role of regulatory commissions, see Marver Bernstein, *Regulating Business by Independent Commission* (Princeton, N.J.: Princeton University Press, 1955); for the Act see Herbert Hovenkamp, *The Federal Trade Commission and the Sherman Act*, Bayard Wickliffe Heath Memorial Lecture (Gainesville: University of Florida, 2010).

2 Craig N. Murphy and JoAnne Yates, *The International Organization for Standardization (ISO): Global Governance through Voluntary Consensus* (London: Routledge, 2009), 5–17. These organizations addressed different customer issues, and much later they came to include consumer participation.

3 However, international business began organizing parts of regulation before the emergence of the International Maritime Organization (IMO) in 1947. Karsten Ronit, "Leading and Following: Private and Public Organizations in the Evolution of Global Shipping," in *Organized Business and the New Global Order*, eds Justin Greenwood and Henry Jacek (London: Macmillan, 2000), 192–203. In the early days the International Maritime Committee (IMC) was an important entity in private regulation.

4 F.S. Northedge, *The League of Nations: Its Life and Times, 1920–1946* (New York: Holmes & Meier, 1986).

5 Bob Reinalda, *Routledge History of International Organizations: From 1815 to the Present Day* (London: Routledge, 2009), 248–9.

6 Lyman Cromwell White, *The Structure of Private International Organizations* (Philadelphia, Penn.: Ferguson, 1933); F.S.L. Lyons, *Internationalism in Europe 1815–1914* (Leiden: A.W. Sythoff, 1963).

7 This issue was relevant and was discussed in countries where the labor movement had gained some strength. Matthew Hilton, *Consumerism in 20th-century Britain* (Cambridge: Cambridge University Press, 2003).

8 Charles Hodges, *The Background of International Relations. Our World Horizons: National and International* (New York: John Wiley, 1931), 360–91.

9 The ICC Code on Advertising was first adopted in 1937 and has since been revised and expanded many times. ICC, *Advertising and Marketing Communication Practice. Consolidated ICC Code* (Document No. 240-46/660) (Paris: International Chamber of Commerce, 2011).

10 Depending on the specialized field of consumer policy, reference was made not only to consumers in general, but also, for instance, to passengers and patients (see Chapter 3).

11 "Consumers" are explicitly mentioned in the text, article IX, 2 and XI, 2 ii, but more as a group to be protected than to be empowered, www.wto.org/english/docs_e/legal_e/gatt47_e.pdf.

12 Lyman Cromwell White, *International Non-governmental Organizations: Their Purposes, Methods, and Accomplishments* (New Brunswick, N.J.: Rutgers University Press, 1951); J.J. Lador-Lederer, *International Non-Governmental Organizations and Economic Entities: A Study in Autonomous Organization and Ius Gentiu* (Leiden: A.W. Sythoff, 1962). For later explorations of the formal relations see, for instance, Peter Willets, *"The Conscience of the World": The Influence of Non-Governmental Organizations in the UN System* (Washington, DC: Brookings Institution Press, 1996); Sergey Ripinsky and Peter Van den Bossche, *NGO Involvement in International Organizations* (London: British Institute of International and Comparative Law, 2007).

13 UN, *Charter of the United Nations and Statute of the International Court of Justice* (New York: United Nations, 1945). The charter, in article 71, referred to ECOSOC's relations with non-governmental organizations: "The Economic and Social Council may make suitable arrangements for consultation with non-governmental organizations which are concerned with matters within its competence."

14 For some traits of this historical asymmetry see, for instance, Kees van der Pijl, *Transnational Classes and International Relations* (London: Routledge, 1998), and for the maintenance of this order see, for instance, Doris Fuchs, *Understanding Business Power in Global Governance* (Baden-Baden: Nomos, 2005).

15 Peter Willetts, *Non-Governmental Organizations in World Politics. The Construction of Global Governance* (London: Routledge, 2011), 12.

16 John F. Kennedy, *Special Message to the Congress on Protecting the Consumer Interest*, March 15, 1962. Online by Gerhard Peters and John T. Woolley, *The American Presidency Project*, www.presidency.ucsb.edu/ws/?pid=9108. In this message, the role of consumers in the American economy

was acknowledged, and important measures to advance their rights were established. Four essential rights were defined: the right to safety, the right to be informed, the right to choose and the right to be heard.

17 Mathew Hilton, "The death of a consumer society," *Transactions of the Royal Historical Society* 18 (2008): 211–36.

18 Foo Gaik Sim, *IOCU on Record: A Documentary History of the International Organization of Consumers Unions, 1960–1990* (Yonkers, NY: Consumers Union, 1991). The IOCU changed its name to Consumers International (CI) in 1995.

19 Tagi Sagafi-Nejad and John Dunning, *From Code of Conduct to Global Compact* (Bloomington: Indiana University Press, 2008).

20 UN, *Multinational Corporations and World Development* (New York: United Nations, 1973).

21 OECD, *OECD Guidelines for Multinational Enterprises* (Paris: Organisation for Economic Co-operation and Development, 1976).

22 UN, *Resolution Adopted by the General Assembly 3201 (S-VI). Declaration on the Establishment of a New International Economic Order*, A/RES/S-6/3201, 1 May 1974.

23 UN, *Charter of Economic Rights and Duties of States*, A/RES/29/3281, article 28.

24 UN, *Resolution Adopted by the General Assembly. Resolution 35/63 of 5 December 1980. The Set of Multilaterally Agreed Equitable Principles and Rules for the Control of Restrictive Business Practices*, IV, section A, 3.

25 UN, *Resolution Adopted by the General Assembly*. Resolution A/RES/39/248 of 16 April 1985. As discussed later, "sustainability" was added in the 1999 revision of the UN Guidelines for Consumer Protection.

26 The Guidelines for Consumer Protection list both "objectives," which are cited here, and "general principles." These are slightly overlapping and the presentation is somewhat inconsequential. See UN, "Expansion of the United Nations guidelines on consumer protection to include sustainable consumption," Resolution 1999/7, United Nations Economic and Social Council, New York, www.un.org/documents/ecosoc/res/1999/eres1999-7.htm.

27 Following the UN Guidelines, legislation was passed on consumer protection in these countries, e.g. *Law of the People's Republic of China on Protecting Consumers' Rights and Interests, adopted by the fourth meeting of the eighth National People's Congress Standing Committee on 31st October 1993*, www.npc.gov.cn/englishnpc/Law/2007-12/12/content_1383812.htm.

28 In the EU, a special consumer body involving consumer organizations – the Consumer Committee – was established in 1975, and a new Directorate-General, DG SANCO, under the presidency of Prodi, emphasized the greater role attributed to consumer policy in the EU. Australian and New Zealand consumer policy was coordinated through the Ministerial Council on Consumer Affairs (MCCA) and various subcommittees, www.consumerlaw.gov.au/content/Content.aspx?doc=ministerial_council.htm.   Throughout the 1990s, consumer protection spread across the Latin American and Caribbean countries. Jean Michel Arrighi, "Integration and consumer protection: the case of Latin America," *Journal of Consumer Policy* 15, no. 2 (1992): 179–90.

29 UN Commission on Global Governance, *Our Global Neighborhood: The Report of the Commission on Global Governance* (Oxford: Oxford University Press, 1995).
30 Amrita Narlikar, *The World Trade Organization* (Oxford: Oxford University Press, 2005), 133–8.

2　General organizations and issues

- Socio-economic organizations
- Trade and development organizations
- Environmental organizations
- Conclusion

A number of intergovernmental agencies focus on general consumer issues. In these contexts, broader ideas, principles and regulations are discussed and adopted without being closely related to any particular industry, commodity or segment of consumers. Beyond the UN and ECOSOC, these bodies include major agencies such as the OECD, World Bank, IMF, WTO, UNCTAD, ISO, ICPEN and UNEP. Notwithstanding the different nature of these organizations, they all tend to table consumer policy in a general way, but individual mandates and orientations color their approaches to this cross-cutting field, and some also explore issues addressed by the specialized organizations studied in Chapter 3. In each organization there will also be alliances of member states and different interested parties that offer their ideas about how consumer policy should be addressed and how it should be balanced with other concerns.

Consumer policy is not the traditional stronghold of these bodies, nor do they always label otherwise consumer-relevant activities as consumer policy, but many regulations have a bearing on consumers, as shown for instance by the OECD Guidelines for Multinational Enterprises. In other words, consumer concerns must find a place among the core and institutionally well established policies such as competition policy, economic policy, trade policy, social policy, environmental policy, development policy and many more. In this chapter we simplify these tasks and distinguish three major types of general organization with backgrounds in the socio-economic, development and trade, and environment fields. Each of these organizations plays an important part in the evolution of global consumer policy, but if no general principles are adopted to guide their activities, there is a risk that strategies become fragmented or perhaps even compete, to the detriment of consumers. We are therefore interested in analyzing attempts to address a number of common problems, foster a unified approach across the various bodies, and transfer experiences across these organizations. Part of this work is further organized in collaboration with other agencies, and we address this dimension in Chapter 4 on inter-agency coordination.

Policy transfer is often analyzed in an international–national optic where internationalization impacts on national institutions and spurs change at this level, an issue that has attracted scholarly attention. However, there is also potential for policy transfer across intergovernmental organizations as they concentrate on either some of the same issues or neighboring areas, which in one way or another may generate learning and transfer policy across institutional boundaries. There may also be hierarchy among international organizations, for instance because of their different and expanding mandates and because of their pioneering experiences with consumer policy, hence their authority to formulate strategies. This is a pertinent issue among the general organizations examined in this chapter.

On top of that, separate entities are created in some of the general organizations to better host the consumer dimension and display a stronger concern for consumers. These units have different functions: compile data, analyze problems, disseminate information and prepare rules; but they also exchange with interested parties including business and the consumer movement, and thus have various consultation functions. One principle that has gained prominence in the work of many intergovernmental organizations is the ambition to draw different kinds of stakeholders more closely into their policy-making structures. Intergovernmental organizations devoting part of their energy to consumer issues are no exception. They institutionalize participation, and they do not adopt policies on the basis of input delivered by member states alone but also include different private stakeholders. Organizations hereby intend to enhance their legitimacy and effectiveness by changing practices and inviting a variety of private organizations into their deliberations. It will be interesting to examine how such governance strategies have evolved with regard to general consumer issues.

Socio-economic organizations

In a number of areas we find a single intergovernmental agency that acts as the flagship organization and seeks to move the relevant policy field forward. In the case of consumer policy, however, we do not find a central organization with such a commitment. Among states, there has never been a strong enough interest in elevating the field to this status and having a permanent and encompassing body to manage consumer affairs. The dominant strategy is to have consumer concerns integrated into, and taken care of by, multiple organizations and through other and adjacent policies. Under these circumstances, the consumer cause has found its way into some general organizations, where the overall principles of consumer protection are discussed and approved. In principle, some forms of policy transfer across organizations are possible, but a barrier is that the socio-economic organizations cater to different constituencies and include different concerns in their approaches to consumer protection.

UN and ECOSOC: a traditional core

With its unique and broad mandate, the United Nations (UN) is a logical platform for addressing socio-economic problems, while it also has a complex structure enabling it to manage many traditional issues and handle new challenges that either are embraced by other organizations or are neglected and therefore deserve a special effort in "filling a gap." At the forefront we find the UN General Assembly, including its various committees, as the representative top body of the organization, and in this policy-making forum consumer affairs are occasionally included and relevant resolutions are adopted. Much work, however, is placed under the auspices of the more specialized Economic and Social Committee (ECOSOC), a body that has been part of the UN from the start.[1] ECOSOC performs many tasks, and consumer affairs must share attention with many other issues. These different bodies are supported by a secretariat, the UN Department of Economic and Social Affairs (DESA), and also the Statistics Division which, for instance, produces data on consumer prices and consumer goods and seeks to standardize and coordinate statistical activity in the UN. In the UN system, however, it is the International Labour Organization (ILO) that is responsible for managing the consumer price indexes and defining relevant standards. This work began in the 1920s and is continually being updated, leading to revisions of the international guidelines on consumer price index and the related ILO manuals.[2] It is an area where consumer policy meets social policy.

An important feature of ECOSOC is its relations with many non-governmental organizations. This body was designed to include a rich variety of non-governmental organizations active in economic and social domains, and both business and consumers plus many other interest categories are represented on the committee. This gives organized consumers good opportunities to influence its work, and the IOCU – and later CI – came to play a vital role as the encompassing association for consumers. Interestingly, ECOSOC is largely designed to manage general issues and not encroach on the many special agencies of the UN, but it can support them in various ways. It is therefore an appropriate forum for addressing general consumer policy, but to some extent issues pertaining to the turf of other agencies are unavoidably addressed, and sometimes this can solidify the efforts of the special agencies. However, the general commitment of ECOSOC corresponds with the profile of the IOCU, which is dedicated to representing consumers in basically all cross-cutting issues, but which also has the capacity to engage in specific sectors, as discussed later.

On various occasions the UN and ECOSOC have been the key forums for the deliberation of general strategies to improve the conditions of consumers, also with a view to changing broader economic structures in the world. The most systematic effort, bringing together many experiences and ambitions, was launched with the UN Guidelines for Consumer Protection, approved by the General Assembly in 1985. This initiative entailed many specified goals that are of general relevance to consumers, and which are therefore transposable to many different sectors.[3] However, the work on the guidelines did not end with this novel initiative. Recent decades have been characterized by implementation of the guidelines in national legislation and evaluation of the different experiences.[4] In the meantime, consumption has progressively become linked with sustainability issues, and provisions on sustainable consumption were added to the guidelines in 1999.[5] This revision recognizes that consumer concerns need to be combined with other goals in public policy, and that consumers should be able to make informed choices and consider the environmental consequences of production and consumption. Different resources should be harnessed: "Responsibility for sustainable consumption is shared by all members and organizations of society, with informed consumers, Government, business, labor organizations, and consumer and environmental organizations playing particularly important roles."[6] Since then, attention to environmental issues has not diminished – on the contrary, it has intensified – and this offers various opportunities for expanding the guidelines in new directions and reinterpreting the goals of consumer policy.

In view of the institutional deficits in general consumer policy, where no consumer agency is available, the work on the guidelines cemented the leading position of the UN, and for a while also that of ECOSOC, as the appropriate forum for negotiating and adopting general consumer principles. However, in light of new demands for consumer rights in areas not covered by the guidelines, the inadequacy of the guidelines became apparent leading to calls for updating. Parallel initiatives to address and expand some of the guideline principles were made in other intergovernmental organizations, such as the OECD – and we will return to these efforts – but the UN guidelines also needed to be thoroughly revised. UNCTAD began to coordinate the revision of the guidelines in 2010–2012, indicating that the division of labor between the various UN bodies is not fixed in the field of consumer policy; indeed, some kind of institutional bricolage is characteristic of this reform process. UNCTAD has played a significant role in the preparation of other initiatives of relevance to consumers, so in many ways this new engagement makes sense.

OECD: a strong tradition

Another major intergovernmental body engaged in a range of social and economic issues is the Organisation for Economic Co-operation and Development (OECD), once a more regional organization but now increasingly global, drawing members from different continents. With a historical baggage heavily loaded with general economic problems, trade and competition, it took some time to incorporate consumer policy.

Like the UN, the OECD is also engaged in consumer policy at a general level and in fact gives considerable attention to this field, following up developments in other organizations and launching its own initiatives. Some weak elements of policy transfer are visible here. It is fair to say that consumer policy has in many ways become more institutionalized and differentiated than in the UN, but its work does not pertain to the situation in developing countries, although some non-member countries from the developing world participate in deliberations on an observer basis.

The OECD has a rich tradition in consumer policy and is not merely engaged under the somewhat diffuse label of competition policy, but actively addresses issues in terms of consumer policy, which is an enabling factor for involving and empowering the consumer movement. In this way the work of the OECD logically reflects the many experiences with consumer regulation in its member countries and the highly institutionalized consumer policy and comparatively high level of consumer protection in the more affluent parts of the world. In a wider perspective, this offers the OECD a special opportunity to inspire other intergovernmental organizations and influence their principles and practices in consumer policy. The organization, along with its staff, is seen as very adept in fostering new ideas and moving into new policy fields. To some degree this activity can be seen as an example of bureaucratic politics to win new turf or as constructivist ability to define agendas,[7] but it is important to emphasize that its many activities are rooted in actual administrative and political experiences with consumer policy in its constituency.

As the core consumer-oriented body, the OECD established its Committee on Consumer Policy (CCP) in 1969, at a time when the international consumer cause gained momentum, and consultation with the consumer movement and other stakeholders is a cornerstone of its work. This forum provides an important opportunity for consumers to voice their concerns, but the creation of the committee must also be seen as an attempt to counterbalance the influence of business on the organization more generally, and as part of an ongoing reform process.[8] The CCP has a unique position, and as the OECD itself stresses: "The CCP is the only intergovernmental forum addressing a broad range of consumer issues. It aims to help public authorities enhance the development of effective consumer policies."[9] This position may be important in different international contexts: experiences with consumer participation can be a lever for introducing and improving consumer participation in other intergovernmental bodies, and strong agendas and strategies initiated in the OECD framework can influence the work of other agencies where consumer policy is less developed.

The CCP has a broad mandate and is supported by the directorates of the OECD secretariat and the Information, Communications and Consumer Policy Division, which examine many consumer issues and provide analyses and data on the basis of research. The committee hosts meetings and workshops on consumer protection, and provides a place for work on a number of guidelines and recommendations which are adopted by the OECD Council. These policies typically cover general issues of relevance to all consumers and, to some extent, to all sectors of the economy, but some regulations pertain to relations between specific groups of consumers and business. The OECD has been a pioneer in electronic commerce and new forms of communication, and has seized the opportunity to advance consumer regulation in new areas. Table 2.1 illustrates the initiatives taken to address consumer issues through various types of guidance.

While the CCP is the major body designated to manage consumer affairs, other entities in the OECD are making inroads into consumer

Table 2.1 OECD guidelines, recommendations and standards in different areas of consumer policy

Type and field of OECD guidelines	Year
Guidance on Intangible Digital Content Products	2014
Recommendation on Consumer Policy Decision Making	2014
Policy Guidance on Mobile and Online Payments	2014
Recommendations on Environmental Claims	2010
Recommendations on Consumer Education	2009
Good Practices on Financial Education and Awareness Relating to Credit	2009
Good Practices for Enhanced Risk Awareness and Education on Insurance Issues	2008
Good Practices for Financial Education Relating to Private Pensions	2008
Policy Guidance on Online Identity Theft	2008
Policy Guidance for Addressing Emerging Consumer Protection and Empowerment Issues in Mobile Commerce	2008
Policy Guidance for Protecting and Empowering Consumers in Communication Services	2008
Recommendation on Consumer Dispute Resolution and Redress (domestic and cross-border issues)	2007
Recommendation on Cross-border Co-operation in the Enforcement of Laws Against Spam	2006
Principles and Good Practices for Financial Education and Awareness	2005
Guidelines for Protecting Consumers from Fraudulent and Deceptive Commercial Practices Across Borders	2003
Guidelines for Consumer Protection in the Context of Electronic Commerce	1999
Recommendation on the Notification System on Consumer Safety Measures	1989
Guidelines for Multinational Enterprises	1976

Source: www.oecd.org/sti/consumer.

policy and taking up issues that are not exclusively consumer-related, but that definitely have a bearing on the conditions of consumers. A prominent example is regulation of the role of multinational enterprises in the global economy, which became an important theme in the 1970s and has since been closely followed and updated by the OECD. The key document is the OECD Guidelines for Multinational Enterprises, adopted in 1976 as part of a larger package on MNE regulation and reviewed on a number of occasions. Especially in the 1980s, consumer interests were integrated into the document, and later other issues, such as human rights, environmental concerns and supply-chain responsibility, were addressed to modernize the guidelines and respond to new and dynamic consumer demands. Even with the latest changes to the guidelines in 2011,[10] however, they remain a set of recommendations to the enterprises and are therefore an example of soft regulation. The guidelines can be seen as an attempt to set important consumer agendas and stress the special responsibility of large corporations, but they can also be interpreted as a strategy to forestall stricter regulation and interference with business authority. Indeed, the original initiative was in part intended to influence the parallel processes in the UN, where developing countries were pressing for regulation, and, from a business perspective, to have the debate in the institutional framework of the OECD. There are therefore different drivers for policy transfer and they are used differently by affected interests.

The Washington institutions – World Bank and IMF: more recent engagement

The OECD focuses on many general socio-economic problems, whereas the two Washington institutions, the World Bank and the International Monetary Fund (IMF), also address a range of questions, partly in other fields, and with their wider global coverage they are committed to taking up issues that are relevant to affluent and developing countries alike. Both organizations seek to shape the general economic and social conditions in their member countries, and thus set very broad growth and development agendas. Consumer policy is not their real departure, however, and they have not had special offices or divisions to direct their activities in consumer affairs. Nor do they have a tradition of consulting with the consumer movement, and they have been criticized for closed and non-transparent decision-making, often to the benefit of business. This image is hard to eradicate, and although an effort is made to improve relations with civil society groups, consumer organizations have not been major exchange partners of the two organizations.[11]

Today the World Bank and the IMF take a more active stance and embrace certain aspects of consumer policy. For the World Bank, and also the IMF, it is logical to pursue broader financial issues, some of which are highly pertinent to all consumers, except perhaps for those parts of the population that are unbanked or in other ways are unrelated to the financial industries, as many people in developing countries still are. By addressing certain areas of financial regulation, however, the World Bank and IMF invariably engage in a kind of sector politics because some of their strategies are targeted at specific industries, such as banking, insurance or pensions. This targeting shows that it is sometimes hard to separate general from specific intergovernmental organizations in the area of consumer policy.

The World Bank engages in different research activities to review the conditions of households on the demand side, and firms on the supply side, of the economy. Relatedly, the organization monitors developments in its member countries and examines how they meet international standards, and it offers various services to amend institutional frameworks with the explicit goal of enhancing financial consumer protection. A global survey on consumer protection with regard to deposit and credit services was carried out in 2013, and more surveys on other consumer issues in the financial industries are now being prepared.[12]

A prerequisite for achieving better protection is to educate consumers and improve their financial literacy, provide information, and give them access to various financial services. Many consumers lack the required knowledge to make an informed choice in this complex field, and many countries lack adequate financial infrastructure to support their necessary education and build trust. Public sector involvement is consequently needed to provide such institutional infrastructures but also assistance from the private sector is encouraged, a point we will return to later.

In this context, it is important to emphasize that improving the financial literacy of consumers is associated with the more general task of educating consumers, a challenge also stated in the UN Guidelines for Consumer Protection. As the primary body responsible for developing this dimension of consumer policy, the United Nations Educational, Scientific and Cultural Organization (UNESCO) gives significant priority to consumer education in a broad sense, and the consumer movement has comparatively strong ties with UNESCO.[13] Today consumer education involves questions such as development, health and sustainability; a so-called teaching module developed by UNESCO states that "traditionally, consumer education was seen as the study of prudent shopping habits, family budgeting, and ways of avoiding advertising and credit traps. However, consumerism touches on all aspects of daily life in the modern world and might be seen as a core value in the North and, increasingly, throughout the South as well."[14]

Of course, certain aspects of consumer education are dealt with by other organizations, and some activities are influenced by specific events. Prompted by the financial crisis, the World Bank has carefully examined existing practices and identified significant gaps in regulation. On the basis of an encompassing report, a set of Good Practices for Financial Consumer Protection has been formulated, proposing no fewer than 39 standards as future benchmarks.[15] Interestingly, these common goals are framed in the language of consumer policy, but they form part of a larger program on financial inclusion to make markets more efficient, bolster the role of the private sector and, in a wider perspective, foster economic growth, particularly in developing countries. Financial consumer protection is therefore clearly anchored in the general mandate of the World Bank, but a more active approach has included issues that lay idle in the past.

The issue of financial consumer protection has alerted a number of other organizations in addition to the World Bank, including the OECD, IMF and G20. Measures are much needed in this previously neglected but today salient field of financial consumer protection. This requires inter-agency coordination between existing organizations, but it also leads to the creation of new bodies.

The IMF has also added some new consumer dimensions to its work, but it is not active in exactly the same areas and to the same degree as the World Bank. Together with the World Bank, however, the IMF works to develop international standards and codes which refer to different clusters of issues, such as policy transparency, financial sector regulation and supervision, and institutional and market infrastructure.[16] Some of these rules are highly relevant to consumers and regulate the behavior of business and government institutions. They are either adopted by the two organizations or approved in other forums, such as the Basel Committee on Banking Supervision (BCBS), under the Bank for International Settlements (BIS), which receives policy input from the World Bank and the IMF. This applies, for instance, to the Core Principles for Effective Banking Supervision.

The IMF is involved in economic surveillance and in providing macro-economic and financial data, including data on consumer prices and consumption, to help governments standardize data needed for drawing up policies. The consumer dimension therefore tends to be integrated into other macro-economic perspectives, and none of the departments of the organization has a specific focus on consumer affairs. Some distinct consumer-related activities can be noted, however. In 2009, the IMF launched the "Access to Finance Project" to gather data on access to basic consumer financial services,[17] an initiative based on a proposal from the UN Advisors Group on Inclusive Financial Sectors. Such activities are related to efforts of the World Bank and other intergovernmental bodies, and are discussed in Chapter 4.

Trade and development organizations

Consumer concerns are intrinsically linked to trade and development issues, and different approaches to handling consumer affairs are found in the typical trade and development organizations. Usually consumer issues are integrated and subordinated under other traditional and dominant agendas, but they may also receive explicit attention. Major intergovernmental agencies that are active in trade and development in one way or another, and that also take up consumer problems, encompass organizations such as WTO, UNCTAD, ISO, ICPEN and WIPO. These organizations do not engage in the regulation of specific industries, but address business in rather general ways, and their consumer-related activities also speak to consumers in general. Because some of the organizations have parallel agendas, certain degrees of policy transfer are possible.

WTO: consumer policy on the sideline

Regulating a significant part of global trade, the World Trade Organization (WTO) is without doubt the most influential organization and the most important forum for negotiating international trade policy. As its name suggests, the lowering of customs and other trade barriers is the guiding and irrevocable paradigm of the WTO, and little space is available for other approaches. Free trade is seen as ultimately benefitting the world's consumers, and consumer protection is rarely mentioned as such. However, critical voices from the consumer movement hold that competition issues should be given greater attention, and the movement further argues that competition is constrained by various restrictive business practices, not least those adopted by large global corporations.[18]

Increasing cross-border operations in business have not been accompanied by sufficient measures to avoid anti-competitive practices, but competition became a stronger theme in the context of the WTO when the issue was formally recognized at the WTO meeting in Doha 2001. However, the Working Group on the Interaction between Trade and Competition Policy (WGTCP) that was set up in 1996 has remained inactive since 2004, so currently there is no organizational entity in the WTO secretariat that explicitly caters to consumer concerns, although it is active in many other ways.[19] Therefore the negotiations in the Doha Round do not include the competition issue, which means that this lever is not available to the consumer movement, and hence there are fewer opportunities to raise consumer concerns as part of a general competition agenda. The language of competition policy is much more amenable to an institution like the WTO, and addressing the core negotiations on trade is much more difficult from the perspective of consumer policy alone. Many competition issues are raised by other organizations that have relations with the WTO, including the OECD and UNCTAD, but maybe there is a chance to reactivate the dimension of consumer policy after the Doha Round.

The WTO is not just an organization that concentrates on general rules governing trade; it also addresses a range of specific issues, markets and commodities, including agricultural products and information technology. Thus the WTO as a general trade organization is also a forum for discussions and negotiations around trade barriers that pertain to specific industries.

One such area is agriculture, which has yielded an Agreement on Agriculture. Issues on food security played a significant role in the Bali Package, concluded in 2013. Food security is of crucial importance for consumers, and when trade barriers are lowered this concern must not be ignored. There is a strong tradition of addressing security to eradicate hunger, especially since the World Summit on Food Security in 1996, which linked trade with development, and other intergovernmental agencies are involved in this issue as well.

Another area concerns information technology. Different opinions prevailed among the member states with regard to including consumer products in negotiations on the tariffs on information technology. Some countries, for instance those in Asia, favored the inclusion of a number of consumer products into the Information Technology Agreement (ITA) concluded in 1996, while others, such as the EU countries, were more hesitant or opposed this strategy.[20] A compromise was found, more countries have joined, and today implementation of the amended agreement is monitored by the WTO's ITA Committee. Trade, development and innovation are important objectives underlying the agreement, but there is also a consumer dimension, although it is not well articulated.

UNCTAD: a central place

While consumer protection is rarely explicitly addressed by the WTO, the United Nations Conference on Trade and Development (UNCTAD) is highly vocal in the field and delivers quite a different story.[21] There is a long tradition of embracing consumer concerns, and especially linking consumer protection with competition, development and trade issues, a pattern quite different from that found in the WTO. UNCTAD also has a clear focus on North–South issues in global trade and the special problems of developing countries.[22]

Considerable weight is given to competition policy, and over the years UNCTAD has been very active in scrutinizing the power of multinational corporations and devising a variety of rules to alter existing business practices. Although these rules are typically issued as non-binding recommendations, and illustrate the difficulties associated with the regulation of global business, their importance should not be underestimated. Interestingly, competition policy does not travel alone in UNCTAD but is combined with consumer policy. Consumer protection and competition policy are listed as some of the key activities of the organization, and corresponding with that we find a unit on "Competition and Consumer Policies" under its Division on International Trade in Goods and Services, and Commodities (DITC). This indicates that consumer concerns are not only attended to in terms of competition policy, but forcefully addressed through the language of consumer protection.

However, the engagement of UNCTAD is not reducible to these few, albeit important, linkages. Its role and ambition are much broader and in many ways comparable with those of the general socio-economic organizations already discussed. Thus UNCTAD, mindful of its special commitment to development, takes up consumer issues in ways similar to those of ECOSOC and the OECD, and it must combine different perspectives on trade, development and poverty reduction.[23] While these other organizations address a number of development issues, UNCTAD has also expanded its activities and moved into areas beyond trade and development. UNCTAD even seems to have taken over some of the responsibilities that formerly lay in ECOSOC. In 2000 a UN conference on restrictive business practices encouraged UNCTAD to convene an expert meeting on consumer policy, and:

> In order to build on the work already accomplished by the United Nations in the area of consumer protection, it was decided that the expert meeting should be guided in its deliberations and recommendations by the UN Guidelines for Consumer Protection. It was also agreed that the Expert Meeting should focus on identifying measures that could lead to more effective implementation of the provisions contained in these guidelines.[24]

While consumer protection in the developing world has always been a focal point, the UN guidelines have a general character, and tasked with the overall monitoring of their implementation, UNCTAD has clearly become involved in broader concerns than trade and development. As discussed below, in 2012 UNCTAD was commissioned to undertake a major revision of the UN Guidelines for Consumer Protection because a through investigation of experiences was needed to make improvements and identify new issues, such as e-commerce and financial services, not covered by the existing guidelines.[25] The comprehensive implementation report has drawn together experiences from many countries and also interested parties such as CI and ICC, and important changes in the guidelines, which are currently negotiated, are envisaged.[26] In the review process the whole lifetime of the guidelines has been examined, not just a fragment with relevance just to trade and development, and the revision of the guidelines as a whole is entrusted to UNCTAD as the central body. The guidelines are still administered by the UN, but in a different organizational framework than in the past.

Clearly, the consumer movement has delivered important inputs into these processes and has quite amicable relations with UNCTAD. Right from its beginning, UNCTAD has placed great emphasis on consultations with relevant non-governmental organizations within its policy domain, and rules for accrediting observer organizations are established. Cooperation with non-governmental organizations is an important element in UNCTAD's strategy, and important information and interests are channeled into its daily work and into the various conferences hosted by the organization. This enables the building of alliances with a rich variety of affected interests, including consumer organizations such as CI, which for many years has enjoyed consultative status as a representative organization for consumers worldwide. The inclusion of civil society must be seen as a counterweight to the influence of business in other organizations, such as the WTO, which is seen as very welcoming to corporate interests, especially those from developed countries.[27] Over the years, UNCTAD has been highly critical of various restrictive business practices, and is a key forum for scrutinizing the power of multinational corporations and a platform for formulating proposals to reorganize the global economy.

ISO: recognition of consumer concerns

In addition to WTO and UNCTAD, we find a number of other trade-related intergovernmental agencies, but with a narrower scope. Some of these bodies have a role to play in certain areas of consumer policy. Within standardization, a rather specialized field, the International Organization for Standardization (ISO) is a hybrid organization, whose members are not governments, like those described until now, but national standard-setting agencies, some of them public bodies and some private organizations. Dating back to the beginning of the previous century, the IOS was reformed in 1947, and today it is engaged in a tremendous number of activities concerned with standard setting. It has a very broad coverage and works in relation to many different industries,[28] yet there are many sectors of business whose standards are not regulated by ISO, and there are other bodies in the public and private sectors involved in global standardization, some of which we will analyze later.

One might think that such a "technical" organization as ISO would not be able to involve the consumer movement and would only facilitate cooperation with business, but the ISO has a comparatively strong consumer profile. Common standards are very important in facilitating trade, making various products available to consumers and improving their functionality across countries. With almost 20 000 voluntary standards developed, ISO is important in "making the world go round," and standardization combines different aspects of trade, competition and consumer policy, with environment and sustainability concerns also included. The ISO observes the rules negotiated within the framework of WTO, and thus complements its work, but it also refers to the UN Guidelines for Consumer Protection and the work of CI in the field. Likewise, these other organizations recognize the specific contributions of ISO to rule-making in global trade.

In ISO, the consumer movement is not just an actor among many other civil society organizations, but acts together with business as principal partners, representing one side of the market. As key stakeholders, consumers dispose of important knowledge to filter into the standardization work of ISO, and they are offered various opportunities to influence standards adopted by the organization.

ISO is a quasi-intergovernmental organization with consumer policy clearly mirrored in its formal structure, and consumer participation is hailed as a major principle.[29] The ISO Committee on Consumer Policy (COPOLCO), established in 1978, involves the national standardization bodies in consumer matters but it also has close relations with CI as a global association. In COPOLCO, consultations are made with a view to bringing the consumer perspective into the development and implementation of standards. Several guides have been issued to protect consumers, and the forum is further involved in educating and professionalizing the work of national members of the ISO, also with a view to having competent exchange partners in its work.[30] While COPOLCO is focused on the consumer dimension, more detailed work is carried out in the numerous technical committees that involve different groups of experts and stakeholders, including relevant consumer associations when consumer interests are affected.

ICPEN: consumers in focus

Whereas the ISO is not an intergovernmental organization in the traditional sense, the final organization we deal with in this section, broadly described as trade and development, also has a special character. The International Consumer Protection and Enforcement Network (ICPEN), formed in 1992 as the International Marketing Supervision Network (IMSN), is not intergovernmental in the sense that government delegates meet there, because its members, the national ombudsmen and equivalent schemes and authorities, have a fairly independent status as law enforcement agencies.[31]

ICPEN does not have a permanent and well staffed secretariat like the other organizations we have analyzed. Its secretariat is rotating, so its resources should be seen rather as the ongoing collective effort of the different ombudsmen and the coordination thorough conferences and steering groups. However, it has developed its organization in many ways and added new issues. It derives its strength from being an entirely consumer-focused agency that does not formulate its strategies in terms of trade or competition policy, but as consumer policy proper.

In the early days of ICPEN, members came primarily from the OECD countries, and cooperation has been institutionalized with the OECD in areas of joint interest, such as e-commerce; however, the organization has now expanded and become more global. This corresponds well with ICPEN's ambition to "encourage practical action to prevent cross-border marketing malpractice."[32] This includes sharing experiences in a global economy and facilitating stronger enforcement in a time of increasing cross-border business operations. Therefore activities are not limited to the exchange of information, but also include the development of new national bodies and best practices to improve the work of the different national consumer-protection agencies, efforts to identify breaches in cross-border trade, and finding appropriate remedies to combat such breaches, including the development of improved complaints procedures.

It is important to emphasize that the network has a general scope, and its activities are not restricted to any particular sector of business. But there are a few exceptions to this broad coverage: it does not embrace financial services, a field increasingly approached by the World Bank; and it does not engage in matters of product safety either.[33] It therefore respects the division of labor among the general consumer organizations and fills some of the gaps left by these other organizations.

WIPO: an element in competition policy

The final intergovernmental organization covered in this section on trade and development organizations is the World Intellectual Property Organization (WIPO), whose strategies have a bearing on consumers in general. In many areas, the protection of property rights is essential to the conduct of trade, and much regulation aims at the rights holder on the business side. However, the interests of consumers are also recognized, and a balance of the interests between different market players is sought in regulation.

The tenet of WIPO is to incentivize innovation by protecting certain rights of property holders within designs, patents, trademarks and origins, and even to establish various mechanisms to settle disputes around the interpretation of these rights. This is a kind of business regulation that is embodied in various international treaties and conventions, which also has implications for consumers. Ideally, regulation protects consumers against being lured by inadequate principles and standards. However, there is also the risk that regulation is too protective and therefore becomes a barrier to competition.

In WIPO, the consumer perspective is not attended to by any special entity, however, and consumer concerns are discussed primarily in terms of competition policy, as in many other international trade agencies. Some activities explicitly link competition with consumer issues, as for instance the adoption of the Development Agenda in 2007,[34] which emphasized the impact of intellectual property rights on developing countries and their consumers.

The balance between business interests, including those of large corporations, and consumers is still disputed, for instance with regard to the Agreement on Trade-Related Aspects of Intellectual Property Rights (TRIPS), but also with regard to specific industries and product groups such as pharmaceuticals. Together with around 250 other organizations, CI enjoys observer status with WIPO. It has some leverage on the regulation of intellectual property rights in this and other fields but not to the same degree as business, which is represented by a rich diversity of associations.

Environmental organizations

If we turn our attention toward the diverse group of environmental organizations, we find a significantly growing interest in linking consumption and sustainability – and, unlike the work of many socio-economic and trade and development organizations, the basic rationale behind these organizations is not to strengthen competition or stimulate growth. Instead, sustainability in its various forms is their overarching goal. However, it is noteworthy that sustainability has become such a salient issue that it is not handled by these organizations alone but also by some of the organizations already involved in defining general consumer policy. This may potentially create some complex mechanisms of policy transfer across the many different agencies that, in one way or another, combine consumer policy with sustainability. The UN, including ECOSOC and UNCTAD, and OECD are examples of organizations moving into sustainability and consumer policy, but the sustainability agenda has permeated the strategies of many other agencies since the Rio Earth Summit in 1992. Also, dedicated environmental organizations such as UNEP link environmental and sustainability agendas with consumer policy.

Organizations with broader agendas: also sustainable consumption

The UN and its many subsidiary bodies have moved into environment and sustainability policy and linked this with consumer policy over recent decades. These efforts are essential to galvanizing new approaches in consumer policy, and this offers a range of opportunities for the consumer-cause agenda when travelling with other and sometimes more successful agendas. Therefore we briefly need to revisit the United Nations and the key document, the UN Guidelines for Consumer Protection, to identify these changes. When it was adopted in 1985, the time was still not ripe for addressing sustainability, but the report of the United Nations Commission on Sustainable Development (CSD) in 1997 had a clear spill-over effect on many intergovernmental organizations, which incorporated new goals. Accordingly, the Guidelines were amended in 1999 to include sections on consumption and sustainability.[35] With the current revision of the guidelines taken over by UNCTAD, experiences with consumption and sustainability are debated and sustainability is cemented as one of the focal points in consumer protection.

Beyond the UN system, the combination of sustainability and consumer policy has made its entry into, for instance, the OECD. The OECD is an encompassing organization engaged in many different areas of public policy and also has a long tradition in consumer policy, and it was quick to pick up sustainability and link it with consumption and a number of other policies. Simultaneously with UN efforts, the OECD realized the need to reorganize economies, and by the late 1990s a number of reports had been published to map the situation and formulate recommendations.[36] The goals are not just to protect and offer consumers new opportunities, but to a significant degree to stimulate action on behalf of governments and business. Although consumer protection has high priority, consumer concerns are still very much subordinated to, and understood in the context of, competition policy, and economic policy in a wider perspective.

The inclusion of sustainability in consumer-focused strategies has clearly added new perspectives to consumer policy, but it has also brought consumer issues much more into the debate on sustainability, and into organizations without a traditional engagement in consumer policy. Because consumption is such an important dimension of how modern societies are organized, environmental organizations need to bring consumption and sustainability together.

The major environmental organizations in consumer policy: influencing consumer choice

There is no single intergovernmental organization that concentrates on all aspects of the environment. Environmental concern is a very fragmented policy field where several organizations are specialized, each in its chosen field of environment and sustainability, and this is indicative of the ways in which environment, sustainability and consumer issues are linked: several environmental organizations allude to consumers and consumption. Competition issues are not highlighted as in many other intergovernmental organizations, and the overarching goal is to enhance sustainable lifestyles. In this context, better information and more choices for consumers are important tools in changing the patterns of production and consumption.

The strategy of the United Nations Environment Programme (UNEP), formed in 1972 and working in lieu of a traditional general organization for the environment, aims to change patterns of production and consumption, and a key point is the education of consumers to adopt new and innovative sustainable lifestyles and facilitate sustainable consumer choices. In 2014 UNEP developed a 10-year framework program on sustainable consumption and production (10YFP), with regard to consumers, to "ensure that relevant, transparent and reliable information on the sustainability of goods and services is provided to facilitate purchasing decisions."[37] CI, along with a few national and regional consumer groups, is involved in this process through a Multi-stakeholder Advisory Committee (MAC) together with governments and business.[38]

The UNEP secretariat has a "production and consumption unit" and has formulated strategies that are applicable to different areas of business, and thus beneficial to consumers in general. In some cases, however, UNEP is also involved in activities with relevance to selected groups of business and consumers, and some activities pertain to specific sections of business, such as the advertising industry and retailers.[39]

The organization also recognizes that sustainable consumption cannot be promoted through intergovernmental organizations alone but also necessitates the active involvement of business, and it encourages the implementation of voluntary standards, and preferably harmonized labels and other tools in business to inform consumers.[40] Many actors in business and civil society, including the consumer movement, have consultative relations with UNEP, but various initiatives of self-regulation are initiated beyond the framework of UNEP and are discussed in Chapter 5.

However, sustainable development has become a salient but difficult issue to manage in practically all environmental areas where the adjoined issues of sustainability *and* consumption are involved. Conferences and commissions on the environment invariably address consumption and how current and future societies can be organized to align growth and sustainable consumption. Notable conferences, such as the United Nations Conference on Environment and Development (UNCED) (Rio de Janeiro, 1992) and the World Summit on Sustainable Development (WSSD) (Johannesburg, 2002), included this issue, and a special effort was made to include business to become part of the solution.[41]

In environmental organizations focused on nature conservation, the orientation toward consumption issues is less visible, but in some organizations with a broader mandate consumption is an important dimension. An example of an environmental organization with a broad agenda, including consumption, is the United Nations Framework Convention on Climate Change (UNFCCC), which is based on a series of annual meetings, the so-called COPs (Conferences of the Parties). The convention has its own secretariat and is thus equipped with an administrative infrastructure akin to other intergovernmental bodies. Another important player and partner in this field is the Intergovernmental Panel on Climate Change (IPCC), an independent body engaged in scientific work and in reaching consensus among scientists. Both organizations are engaged in providing a scientific background for climate policy, and an important strategy in this policy field is to advance sustainable consumption to halt climate change. The real goal is therefore the state of the environment, not the advancement of consumer rights. Although policies are not formulated in the language of consumer policy, it is recognized that consumers play a key role, and that the choice of consumers has a huge impact on sustainable consumption.[42] An important task therefore is to enable consumers to make an informed choice, but in turn this requires new approaches on the side of the business community.

Conclusion

A number of intergovernmental organizations formulate and adopt general rules to protect the interests of consumers. Most of these rules have the character of guidelines, principles and recommendations, and still their effectiveness very much hinges on their domestic implementation, but they have experienced a considerable expansion over recent decades as the consumer dimension has been integrated in different policy fields. This is not least attributable to the participation of the consumer movement in many of these organizations, and it has pushed for a stronger and distinct focus on consumer protection, but participation varies in the different organizations embracing consumer policy.

Because there is no lead agency tasked with consumer affairs alone, several organizations, all with broad policy portfolios, deliver their own inputs into global consumer policy, and they have different approaches depending on their basic mandates and commitments. There is some policy transfer across organizations, and bodies such as ECOSOC, UNCTAD and the OECD have long experience with the formulation of general strategies in consumer protection, which is helpful for other bodies. Countries that prioritize consumer policy can be important catalysts. However, the initiatives of some of the most experienced organizations are seldom followed up by other general organizations in any manifest way, and there is still much mutual neglect. Policy transfer is generally slow and indirect, and more theoretical work is needed to understand the mechanisms of policy transfer between agencies.

We have identified three major categories of agencies and labelled them socio-economic, trade and development, and environmental organizations. These points of departure lead to different interfaces between consumer policy and other policies.

First, a handful of socio-economic agencies with very broad profiles address consumer protection and issue principles to enhance the rights of consumers around the world. Their consumer strategies are to different degrees flanked or even outranked by other goals, in particular competition policy. In the UN and some of its subsidiary bodies, consumer protection is the primary objective, but in other organizations, for instance the OECD, consumer policy is an aspect of competition policy.

Second, a number of intergovernmental organizations frame consumer policy in terms of trade and development policy, but in these contexts competition also matters. However, the focus on the anti-competitive measures of MNCs as a challenge to consumers varies considerably among these organizations. Relatedly, divergence can also be observed with regard to the priority given to consumer issues in the global North and the global South. It is sometimes difficult to separate trade and development from socio-economic organizations, and this applies for instance to UNCTAD, which has taken a lead role in revising the UN Guidelines for Consumer Protection.

Third, a final category of organizations approaches consumer issues from an environmental and sustainability perspective. These organizations and their efforts are of more recent origin and, because agencies tend to concentrate on selected areas, there are also multiple organizations that combine environment and sustainability with consumer affairs. While this category of organizations moves into consumer policy, there are also socio-economic organizations that have a traditional consumer focus, which move into and add new dimensions to consumer protection and consumption issues.

We have analyzed the general organizations and identified major organizations and initiatives, and we can conclude that they tend to relate to consumers – and also business – in a very broad sense. Nevertheless, we have noted in a few cases that the division of labor is not always clear-cut, and some general organizations take up questions of concern to special industries and segments of consumers, for instance the financial industries and their customers. Efforts of this kind, however, are made mainly by a variety of intergovernmental agencies with competence in their own special areas of consumer policy.

Notes

1 Tim Arnold, *Reforming the UN: Its Economic Role* (London: Royal Institute of International Affairs, 1995); Gert Rosenthal, "Economic and Social Council," in *The Oxford Handbook on the United Nations*, eds T. G. Weiss and S. Daws (Oxford: Oxford University Press, 2007), 136–48.

2 ILO, *Revision of the International Guidelines on Consumer Price Index. Background Paper* (Geneva: International Labour Organization, 1999), www.ilo.org/public/english/bureau/stat/guides/cpi/revguid.htm. This work is organized by an inter-agency working group, the Intersecretariat Working Group on Price Statistics (IWGPS), which today involves the following organizations: IMF, United Nations Economic Commission for Europe (UNECE), ILO, OECD, Eurostat and the World Bank. It is not treated in Chapter 4 on inter-agency coordination, where other fields are covered.

3 UN, *United Nations Guidelines for Consumer Protection*, A/RES/39/248, 16 April 1985 (New York: United Nations, 1985). Different views prevail as to the effectiveness of the UN Guidelines: David Harland, "The United Nations Guidelines for Consumer Protection," *Journal of Consumer Policy* 10, no. 3 (1987), 245–66; Murray Weidenbaum, "The case against the UN Guidelines for Consumer Protection," *Journal of Consumer Policy* 10, no. 4 (1987): 425–32.

4 UNCTAD, *Implementation Report: United Nations Guidelines for Consumer Protection (1985–2013)* (draft). Thirteenth session, Geneva, July 2013, http://unctad.org/Sections/ditc_ccpb/docs/UNGCP_Implementation_Report_v1.pdf.

5 UN, *United Nations Guidelines for Consumer Protection* (as expanded in 1999) (New York: United Nations, 2003). For the efforts of various organizations to link sustainability and consumption, see Doris Fuchs and Sylvia Lorek, "Sustainable consumption governance: a history of promises and failures," *Journal of Consumer Policy* 28, no. 3 (2005): 261–88.

6 UN, *United Nations Guidelines for Consumer Protection* (as expanded in 1999), paragraph G 43 (New York: United Nations, 2003).

7 Rianne Mahon and Stephen McBride, eds, *The OECD and Transnational Governance* (Vancouver: University of British Columbia Press, 2009); Richard Woodward, *The Organization for Economic Co-operation and Development (OECD)* (London: Routledge, 2009). This research is important in understanding the role of the OECD in relation to its member countries, but is less significant in analysis of its role in relation to other international agencies.

8 The OECD manages many other committees, some of which have relevance for consumer policy, for instance the Competition Committee. For treatment of the organization and its various reforms see e.g. Rianne Mahon and Stephen McBride, eds, *The OECD and Transnational Governance* (Vancouver: University of British Columbia Press, 2008); Richard Woodward, *The Organisation for Economic Co-operation and Development* (London: Routledge, 2009); Peter Carroll and Aynsley Kellow, *The OECD: A Study of Organisational Adaptation* (Cheltenham: Edward Elgar, 2011).

9 OECD, *Committee on Consumer Policy* (Paris: OECD, 2012), www.oecd.org/internet/consumer/CCP%20brochure.pdf.

10 OECD, *OECD Guidelines for Multinational Enterprises: 2011 Edition* (Paris: OECD, 2011). For an evaluation of these changes see Peter Muchlinski, *The 2011 Revision of the OECD Guidelines for Multinational Enterprises: Human Rights, Supply Chains and the "Due Diligence" Standard for Responsible Business*, A4ID Series on Responsible Business (London: School of Oriental and African Studies, 2011).

11 The same discussion on participation applies to the World Bank and the IMF. Jan Aart Scholte (edited with A. Schnabel), *Civil Society and Global Finance* (London: Routledge, 2002); Jan Aart Scholte, "Civil society and financial markets: what is not happening and why," *Journal of Civil Society* 9, no. 2 (2013): 129–47. For their current strategies see www.imf.org/external/np/exr/cs/index.aspx and http://web.worldbank.org/WBSITE/EXTERNAL/TOPICS/CSO/0,pagePK:220469~theSitePK:228717,00.html.

12 World Bank, *Consumer Protection and Financial Literacy (CPFL)* (Washington, DC: World Bank, 2013). This study addresses issues such as

the legal framework, institutions, disclosure practices, dispute resolution and financial literacy and covers the situation in 114 countries. http://resp onsiblefinance.worldbank.org/surveys/providers-of-financial-services.

13 UNESCO, however, regards the representativeness of Consumers International (CI) as "passable but unbalanced," http://ngo-db.unesco.org/r/or/en/ 1100020545.

14 UNESCO, *Teaching and Learning for a Sustainable Future* (Paris: UNESCO, 2010), Introduction.

15 World Bank, *Good Practices for Financial Consumer Protection* (Washington, DC: World Bank, 2012). In the World Bank, the financial crisis led to an outburst of new initiatives to regulate consumer protection in finance.

16 The Financial Sector Assessment Program (FSAP) was agreed to in 1999 and has since been overhauled. IMF, *Factsheet, FSAP*, 18 March 2014.

17 IMF, *IMF Launches Project to Compile Data on Consumer Access to Basic Financial Services,* Press Release No. 09/351, 5 October 2009.

18 CI, *Consumer Policy and Multilateral Competition Frameworks: A Consumers International Discussion Paper* (London: Consumers International, 2003).

19 Like many intergovernmental organizations, the WTO has put much energy into reforming its institutional structures, and welcomes dialogue with civil society organizations. As with the GATT, its predecessor, the WTO is still being criticized for being elitist, and the larger concern with consumer issues has not led to the creation of overarching consumer-orientated bodies. This literature stresses the weak links with civil society organizations and discusses this problem in relation to broader governance challenges of the organizations. Steve Charnowitz, "Opening the WTO to non-governmental interests," *Fordham International Law Journal* 24, nos 1–2 (2000): 173–216; Daniel C. Esty, "Non-governmental organizations at the World Trade Organization: cooperation, competition, or exclusion," *Journal of International Economic Law* 1, no. 1 (1998): 123–47; Hannah Murphy, *The Making of International Trade Policy: NGOs, Agenda-Setting and the WTO* (Cheltenham: Edward Elgar, 2010).

20 WTO, *15 Years of the Information Technology Agreement Trade, Innovation and Global Production Networks* (Washington, DC: World Trade Organization, 2012).

21 Another branch of the UN, the United Nations Commission on International Trade Law (UNCITRAL), established in 1966, produces a huge number of legislative texts and provides some of the basic rules in trade, but it is not involved in trade negotiations. Gerard McCormack, *Secured Credit and the Harmonisation of Law: The UNCITRAL Experience* (Cheltenham: Edward Elgar, 2011). In UNCITRAL, conventions, guides and recommendations are adopted to regulate global trade, and some of these rules have a so-called b2c (business to consumer) dimension, in which consumer participation is relevant. As with UNCTAD, the UN is not just a highly general organization in which only general principles in consumer policy are outlined.

22 There are distinct North–South differences in the ability to consume. This situation was analyzed in UNDP, *Consumption for Human Development* (New York: UNDP, 1998), and also stressed in the 2014 *Human Development Report.*

23 Jennifer Clapp and Rorden Wilkinson, eds, *Global Governance, Poverty and Inequality. Global Institutions* (London: Routledge, 2010); Rorden Wilkinson and James Scott, eds, *Trade, Poverty, Development* (London: Routledge, 2012).

24 UN, *United Nations Guidelines for Consumer Protection* (as expanded in 1999) (New York and Geneva: United Nations, 2001), iii, http://unctad.org/en/Docs/poditcclpm21.en.pdf.

25 UN, *United Nations Guidelines for Consumer Protection* (as expanded in 1999) (New York: United Nations, 2003), paragraph G 43.

26 UNCTAD, *Implementation Report. United Nations Guidelines for Consumer Protection (1985–2013)*. Intergovernmental Group of Experts on Competition Law and Policy, Thirteenth session, United Nations TD/B/C. I/CLP/ (Geneva: UNCTAD, 2013). http://unctad.org/Sections/ditc_ccpb/docs/UNGCP_Implementation_Report_v1.pdf.

27 UNCTAD, *List of Non-governmental Organizations Participating in the Activities of UNCTAD*, United Nations TD/B/NGO/LIST/16, United Nations Conference on Trade and Development, 11 February 2014.

28 ISO is not a traditional intergovernmental body with states as members, but the status of its members differs with regard to their public and private character. In the scholarly literature, ISO tends to be seen as a non-governmental organization, although it is observed that two-thirds of its members "are part of their country's central government." Craig N. Murphy and JoAnne Yates, *The International Organization for Standardization (ISO), Global Governance through Voluntary Consensus* (London: Routledge, 2009), 25. When analyzing its relations with other organizations, it is interesting to note, however, that the WTO recognizes the ISO as an intergovernmental organization. WTO, *International intergovernmental organizations granted observer status to WTO bodies*, www.wto.org/english/thewto_e/igo_obs_e.htm.

29 ISO/IEC, *ISO/IEC Statement on Consumer Participation in Standardization Work*, ISO/IEC/GEN 01:2001 mj/pc/12554061 (Geneva: ISO/IEC, 2001). These principles were confirmed through COPOLCO resolution 3/2009.

30 ISO, *Standardization Involving Consumers: Why and How* (Geneva: ISO, 2011), www.iso.org/iso/involving_consumers.pdf.

31 Also in competition policy we find a network arrangement. Created in 2001, the International Competition Network (ICN) facilitates cooperation between national competition authorities in many countries, based on consensus. "By enhancing convergence and cooperation, the ICN promotes more efficient and effective antitrust enforcement worldwide for the benefit of consumers and businesses," as the network describes its own efforts. ICN, *ICN Factsheet and Key Messages*, April 2009, 2. www.internationalcompetitionnetwork.org/uploads/library/doc608.pdf.

32 ICPEN, *Memorandum on the Establishment and Operation of the International Consumer Protection and Enforcement Network (ICPEN)*. Memorandum agreed to at the Conference in Jeju – Republic of Korea, 26–28 March 2006.

33 Product safety is addressed by organizations such as the OECD, which already manages many different tasks. A body concentrating on product safety is the International Consumer Product Safety Caucus (ICPSC),

which has members from Australia, Brazil, Canada, China, the European Union, Japan, Korea and the USA.

34 WIPO, *The 45 Adopted Recommendations under the WIPO Development Agenda* (Geneva: WIPO, 2007).

35 UN, *United Nations Guidelines for Consumer Protection* (as expanded in 1999) (New York: United Nations, 2003).

36 Toward the end of the 1990s, the OECD issued many reports on the relationship between consumption and sustainability. OECD, *Sustainable Consumption and Production* (Paris: OECD, 1997); OECD, *Sustainable Consumption and Production: Clarifying the Concepts* (Paris: OECD, 1998); OECD, *Towards Sustainable Consumption Patterns: A Progress Report on Member Country Initiatives* (Paris: OECD, 1999); OECD, *Education and Learning for Sustainable Consumption* (Paris: OECD, 1999).

37 UNEP, *The 10YFP Programme on Consumer Information* (Paris: UNEP, 2014).

38 For a broader picture of civil society involvement, see Anne E. Egelston, *Sustainable Development: A History* (Heidelberg: Springer, 2014).

39 UNEP, *What is Sustainable Consumption?* www.unep.org/resourceeffi ciency/Portals/24147/scp/communications/pdf/ad-brochure.pdf.

40 UNEP sees standards and labels as important tools to inform consumers about sustainable consumption, see www.unep.org/resourceefficiency/ Society/StandardsLabelsandProcurement/tabid/55549/Default.aspx.

41 Interestingly, a new business forum, the World Business Council for Sustainable Development (WBCSD), was formed in connection with the Earth Summit in Rio de Janeiro.

42 Eva Charkiewicz with Sander van Bennekom and Alex Young, *Transitions to Sustainable Production and Consumption* (Maastricht: Shaker, 2001); Laurie Michaelis, "Sustainable consumption and greenhouse gas mitigation," *Climate Policy* 3, Supplement 1 (2013): 135–46.

3 Special organizations and issues

- **WHO: long-standing commitment to patients**
- **FAO: established concern for consumers**
- **ICAO: the somewhat hidden but central role of passengers**
- **ITU: consumer policy subordinate to competition policy**
- **UNWTO: consumer interests combined with other concerns**
- **Conclusion**

All the special consumer organizations have a comparatively narrow focus. They adopt policies that pertain to particular sectors of business, and consumers for their part can only invoke and benefit from regulations of particular industries and markets. Thus they have a different type of mandate than the general organizations involved in global consumer policy but, as with the general organizations, they are not designed to manage consumer issues as their primary task, and consumer policy is often just a minor aspect.

It is important to keep in mind that all these efforts are not isolated from broader endeavors to address consumer concerns. It is only natural that the special organizations follow up and apply rules adopted in the general forums discussed in Chapter 2, but each of the special organizations has its own unique position in consumer policy. The constellation of forces, including the active role taken by relevant consumer and business groups in these subfields, has a huge influence on the activities and directions in these areas of consumer policy. In order to protect consumers, the WHO, for instance, adopts strategies to set norms and standards for companies active in the health sector, such as producers of drugs or medical equipment, but of course not for business in general, and thus very targeted approaches are formulated.

There is no firm, agreed-upon approach for how to distinguish between different categories of intergovernmental organizations in the global arena,[1] but for the purpose of this book we draw a line between organizations engaged in the protection of consumers irrespective of concrete markets, and organizations adopting rules pertaining to business and consumers operating in specific markets. Still there are conceptual difficulties to solve and borderline cases to evaluate. We do, for instance, find organizations involved in the regulation of specific areas of business, such as the financial industries, but the financial industries have a general role in the economy, and regulations influence the conditions of consumers on a very broad basis, so these organizations can be treated as general organizations. We may also find it confusing to see some organizations with a very general approach to consumer policy but which also take an interest in a certain branch of business. This is, for instance, the case in trade, where the WTO adopts and applies rules to regulate particular areas, such as food.

All the organizations analyzed in this chapter are engaged in the formulation of strategies and the adoption of rules that refer to selected areas and specific types or roles of consumers in the main target selected areas of business. The special organizations are active in areas where profound knowledge is required to adopt and implement strategies, and this activity calls for close cooperation with external parties. An interesting debate in the study of intergovernmental organizations concerns the importance of knowledge. In the literature, reference is sometimes made to "epistemic communities," which are seen as accommodating both bureaucratic and professional groups; accordingly, the staff of these agencies may share approaches and beliefs with other kinds of experts. However, external parties may represent both affected interests and independent expertise, thereby bringing new perspectives into the formation of knowledge as a basis for intergovernmental organizations.

We focus attention on some of the main subfields of consumer policy and include the WHO, FAO, ICAO, ITU and UNWTO, all playing a distinctive role with regard to business and consumers. These agencies seek inspiration from the general development of global consumer policy and the many general efforts to enhance consumer protection, but they also have their own distinguishable agendas. We analyze each of these organizations in turn, and conclude the chapter by discussing what characterizes the work of this group of special consumer organizations.

WHO: long-standing commitment to patients

Attention to consumers is emblematic of the World Health Organization (WHO). From its inception in 1946, the organization has kept a clear focus on the health of the individual, and the vision of health has been extended and is "not merely the absence of diseases,"[2] as the title of its current work program stresses, but also addresses well-being in a much broader sense, spanning the struggle against communicable and non-communicable diseases and many other challenges in modern society.

In general, however, the organization does not always refer to consumers, rather to patients or people in connection with the eradication, prevention and treatment of diseases, and therefore concepts such as "patients," "people" or "consumers" are not always used interchangeably. Explicit reference to consumers is made only occasionally,[3] and health professionals do not view people primarily as consumers, at least not in the public sector. Although the vocabulary is somewhat ambiguous and not always consequential, it is possible to draw a line between situations when people are acting on a market and in relation to business, most typically the drug industry, and when people's health concerns are taken care of by the public health sector and there is no traditional market. It is only some key examples under the former dimension that we will attend to here, and because different sections of business play a huge role in relation to, yes, consumers, there are many issues and hence many efforts being made to regulate these markets to protect consumers. These health industries and markets are expanding quite considerably, offering ever new products and treatments to consumers, but definitely not all are addressed by international regulation.

However, many initiatives are developed for the betterment of consumer conditions without necessarily regulating business and setting standards for firms to comply with, although some of these initiatives can bring important inspiration to business as well, for instance the need to amend information strategies. We saw, for instance, that consumer education has become quite a prominent issue in intergovernmental organizations, with a general engagement in consumer policy but with no commitment to specify strategies in relation to particular sectors. In the WHO, broader ideas on consumer education are applied, specific forms of "literacy" are required to make informed choices in a complex and vital area, and consumer education and the rational use of drugs are intrinsically related.[4] The idea of the rational use of drugs was first formulated at the Nairobi Conference of Experts in 1985, but has since been further defined.

The goal to enhance the effective use of medicines in all its dimensions was also expressed in the WHO's Medicines Strategy, first adopted in 1998, and managed by a special entity, the Cluster of Health Systems and Innovation (HIS). The WHO is today making a huge effort to enhance the rational use of drugs, and this involves the different stages of prescribing, dispensing, selling and using medicines.[5] Many activities are launched to assist national health systems and improve their cost-effectiveness, and here the educational element is highly relevant to consumers. Accordingly, a basic goal is to establish "effective medicines information systems to provide independent and unbiased medicine information – including on traditional medicine – to the general public and to improve medicine use by consumers."[6] This concern is built into many activities, mentioned in programs and evaluated in reports, and also addressed in many institutional contexts, for instance at the International Conferences on Improving Use of Medicines (ICIUM), a special forum for non-industrialized countries.

In 2004 WHO adopted the Guidelines on Developing Consumer Information on Proper Use of Traditional, Complementary and Alternative Medicine.[7] These comprehensive and detailed guidelines include much inspiration for governments, and as the guidelines stress, the field "is unregulated in most countries, communication between patients and health care providers is generally poor, and there is an urgent need to develop consumer information in order to minimize the risks and maximize the benefits of [traditional, complementary and alternative medicine.]"[8] These guidelines were elaborated to denote different types of health care providers, and recognized the different sources of medicines that are available today. This also makes the choice of health care harder for consumers.

Consumer information is provided by many different sources, but health care providers, especially the pharmaceutical industry, are important. Accordingly, national and international efforts are made to regulate the industry and its relations with consumers, secure the quality and safety of products, and provide correct information through various forms of labelling and advertising, tasks indicated in the WHO constitution.

In terms of product quality, WHO has issued a Certification Scheme on the Quality of Pharmaceutical Products Moving in International Commerce, supported by guidelines on the implementation of the scheme, which offers a model for national authorities to keep "good manufacturing practices." Already in 1969, the WHO defined principles of good manufacturing practices,[9] and these requirements have been updated on several occasions and work together with other international efforts to inspect and secure product quality.[10] The certification scheme places special emphasis on the responsibility of the exporting country, which is typically, but not always, the developed countries and their global pharmaceutical industries.

Although the quality of products is important, there are further aspects demanding regulation to protect the consumers. Many drugs are directly marketed to consumers, and rules on, for instance, labelling and advertising are therefore needed, but it has proven difficult to keep pace with the marketing activities of the pharmaceutical industry, and much regulation lies with national governments or the industry itself in the form of self-regulation, a point we return to in Chapter 5. Some interesting initiatives, however, have been taken by the WHO, which promotes a variety of guidelines, standards and norms, some of which are important to consumers.

After the Ethical and Scientific Criteria for Pharmaceutical Advertising were adopted by the WHO in 1968, and served as an inspiration for government and industry, work on them was first resumed in the late 1980s, leading to a new and elaborated set of rules. They came to embrace different aspects of marketing (promotion, advertising, packaging and labelling) and were endorsed by the World Health Assembly in 1988.[11] The criteria follow the basic idea of rational use of medicines briefly discussed above. They are meant to serve as an inspiration for all actors who, in one way or another, take an interest in drug promotion, including of course the different manufacturers, distributors and promoters of drugs, as well as the consumers and their organizations.

It is important to note that the criteria "do not constitute legal obligations."[12] In their present form, they cannot be seen as an alternative to self-regulation, but there is some institutional competition as to whether solutions should be sought in a private or a public framework, and whether industry initiatives live up to the ideas contained in the Ethical Criteria. For many years, however, most developments have taken place in business and the Ethical Criteria have not been updated, but problems of weak implementation have been emphasized,[13] also in the discussion on the rational use of drugs. Attempts have been made to monitor this development jointly by the WHO and consumer organizations active in health policy, because they do not see the current situation as satisfactory to consumers.[14] This view is shared by much research, which, however, has focused less on the role of intergovernmental agencies in this process and has been more concerned with the behavior of industry.[15]

Another issue, again relating to the rational use of medicines, but also carrying its own agenda, is the safety of drugs. This is a basic activity the mission of which is to protect patients, and which has long been institutionalized in the WHO. Today this effort is further related to the general WHO safety program, which covers a large number of issues in the meetings between health care systems and patients. Today the core task related to drugs is administered by a special unit, the Quality Assurance and Safety of Medicines (QSM) team, but assistance is also provided from outside the WHO secretariat, for instance through the Uppsala Monitoring Centre (UMC), a WHO Collaborating Centre for International Drug Monitoring, and through different national centers according to the International Drug Monitoring Program dating back to the early 1960s. These activities are supported by the WHO Advisory Committee on Safety of Medicinal Products (ACSoMP), and today various entities collect information and run databases to record and evaluate various cases of adverse drug reaction, the so-called pharmacovigilance.

A significant apparatus in and around the WHO is established to perfect the safety of drugs. Associated with this challenge is the effort to ensure the high quality of drugs and to combat the spread of counterfeit products in international commerce. This problem is of growing concern because much distribution of drugs today is via the internet, a booming market which is very challenging for consumers, and therefore a special problem demanding its own experts and entities to trace such products and take effective measures to halt this development. A special policy, formulated in the Guidelines for the Development of Measures to Combat Counterfeit Drugs,[16] was adopted in 1999, and in 2006 the WHO created a new unit, the International Medical Products Anti-Counterfeiting Taskforce (IMPACT), to follow the situation closely and take appropriate action. This clearly shows that, while there can be problems with the regulation of the traditional industry and the compliance of recognized pharmaceutical companies with various WHO regulations, there is a different section of business that is very difficult to reach but which poses grave problems to consumers worldwide.

Safety is a concern relating to different health care products,[17] and safety matters rank high on the WHO agenda as a vital element in consumer protection. However, safety embraces other products and issues, especially food safety, where the organization has an equally strong tradition of engagement. The WHO delivers important inputs, but strategies on food safety are not managed by the WHO alone, and this shows that the organization and its staff become involved in broader knowledge communities. Because authority is shared with the FAO, and some would see the FAO as the principal body, it is natural to analyze food safety as a core FAO activity – and additionally to examine these activities in the context of inter-agency coordination, as important joint institutions are created in food safety.

FAO: established concern for consumers

As in the WHO, concern for consumers within the Food and Agriculture Organization (FAO) harks back to the organization's foundation in 1945 and is inscribed in its mandate. Although basic FAO documents also refer to the opaque "peoples," different concepts of consumers are generally not employed, which was the case in the WHO, and usually FAO refers just to "consumers." Some of the major goals of FAO are to provide better information to consumers to help them make informed choices and to grant them some essential rights to further protect them. But whereas health care providers in many countries come from the public as well as the private sector, "food providers" are generally a private-sector affair, and food production and processing span a rich variety of industries.

FAO is leveraged by many national, economic and social interests that bring different and sometimes conflicting perspectives into the organization.[18] A risk is that FAO becomes captured by powerful business interests, such as the sugar and tobacco industries, and does not meet consumer demands, so different concerns must be taken into account. This implies that FAO exchanges with an equally varied group of interests, and FAO has elaborated strategies to manage relations, and hammered these principles out in a set of guidelines with the purpose of achieving some kind of balance in the representation of interest groups.[19]

Notwithstanding these different contributions, a basic task is to ensure the accessibility and affordability of food, an overriding concern in many countries, but this goal is rather broad and goes beyond consumer policy in a more traditional sense. It also is related to food security and the right to food and nutrition.[20] As formulated in the Global Strategic Framework for Food Security and Nutrition, "food security exists when all people, at all times, have physical, social and economic access to sufficient, safe and nutritious food that meets their dietary needs and food preferences for an active and healthy life. The four pillars of food security are availability, access, utilization and stability. The nutritional dimension is integral to the concept of food security and to the work of CFS."[21]

In line with these overall strategies, a targeted activity to address consumer concerns is the effort to educate consumers and to enhance the quality and safety of food. Major parts of these activities are today directed by a specialized unit in FAO, the Agriculture and Consumer Protection Department, today one of five departments in the organization, which was established in 2006 with an extended mandate.[22] Other entities are also devoted to consumer affairs, indicating the comparatively strong and explicit attention to consumer issues among intergovernmental organizations.

Over recent decades, FAO has developed strategies to educate people in their role as consumers through activities labelled "nutrition education," an area today administered by a special body in the organization, the Nutrition Education and Consumer Awareness Group under the Nutrition Division, which is again attached to the Economic and Social Development Department in FAO. In other words, FAO assists governments in educating consumers to better understand the complexities underlying the nutritional values of foods and thus achieve a healthier diet. This kind of education is important both in cases where an abundance of food is available, and in cases where food is scarce and undernutrition and various deficits pose a risk, and therefore education needs to be adapted to different environments. FAO activities also account for variations across countries and different consumer segments, such as children and other vulnerable groups, but special energy is devoted to the situation in developing countries which lack sufficient resources and knowledge to further education. Consumer policy is here interwoven with nutrition policy and development policy in a broader perspective, areas where cooperation with other agencies is called for.

The nutritional quality of food is also an important topic in FAO. While consumers can influence quality through raising and specifying demands – and consumer education is a means to that end – it is very much the responsibility of the food industry to improve the quality of food products and provide appropriate information. The self-interest of industry is a key driver for change. However, public policy is also an important tool to influence and examine the quality of various food products. For instance, "the nutritional quality of meat is objective yet 'eating' quality, as perceived by the consumer, is highly subjective,"[23] and some FAO guidelines and manuals instruct on how to handle different steps in the production process, and thus help relevant government authorities and industry to raise standards to the benefit of consumers.

Interestingly, FAO has a strategy to improve quality along the food chain, but this work is focused to a considerable extent on establishing voluntary standards in business. It can be difficult to adopt and monitor rules across such a diverse area of business as the food industry, but it is also a challenge to oppose a strong and determined business community, and therefore FAO gives strong encouragement to the industries to run their own voluntary programs.[24] These standards typically employ different kinds of labels to provide information and to function as quality assurance, alluding to, for instance, the contents of products and the production process. At the same time it can be an advantage for the industry to define and police the standards and thus avoid public regulation at national and international levels, but a central question is whether private standards live up to the general expectations of traditional public regulation.[25]Ample evidence of these highly varied mechanisms of self-regulation will be provided in Chapter 5.

Food quality is intrinsically connected with food safety, and quality and safety matters are managed by the same division of the organization, but safety also involves other entities, some of which are production- rather than consumption-oriented in their work. Safety matters go beyond the issue of quality and involve other and more critical problems for producers as well as for consumers. Some challenges can best be handled at the local or national level, but with the globalization of production and consumption, food safety became a global issue decades ago. Here concerted action through FAO and other agencies is needed and requires much expert knowledge.

Measures to prevent hazards are needed, and should hazards occur, prompt reaction is required to handle ensuing crises and rebuild trust. In principle, food is a type of commodity that is consumed by all consumers all the time, and therefore food safety can be seen as a truly public good, and today a global public good associated with global trade. Typically, a key goal of agencies is to avoid various infections and intoxications, and some diseases that are transmissible from animals to humans have caused great concern.[26] However, some foods may also be contaminated due to scores of factors in the production process and in the environment, a complex issue in modern food production, and one with serious consequences for consumers.[27] It is therefore essential that certain established and scientifically based limits of residues, such as drugs, pesticides and other types of chemical additives, are not exceeded, because such residues may be harmful to humans either in the short or in the long run, and should not be spread along the food chain. This is a great challenge for conventional agriculture.

However, general principles on safety are applied to different foods: meat, dairy and plant products. In relation to these different products, smaller knowledge communities exist and they must continually update data and check procedures. Different kinds of risks are associated with these product categories and call for a variety of procedures to control and inspect production, and codes, guidelines and manuals are adopted to enhance safety. Because food consumption is significantly higher and more diversified in developed countries, given their advanced practices and resources, FAO has a special role to play in relation to food production in developing countries, which have weaker institutions and less access to expert knowledge than affluent countries, and as a consequence both policy advice and technical assistance are provided.

FAO is not the only intergovernmental organization involved in the regulation of food and the setting of food safety standards. A substantial part of consumer policy in relation to food safety is carried out by FAO in cooperation with other agencies, first and foremost with the WHO; thus we return to discussion of the FAO in Chapter 4. While FAO shares responsibility with WHO on the crossroads between food policy and health policy, other agencies are active in special areas of consumer policy without typically sharing authority with others. One of these is ICAO.

ICAO: the somewhat hidden but central role of passengers

Like WHO and FAO, the International Civil Aviation Organization (ICAO), founded in 1947, goes back to the early days of reorganizing international organizations after the Second World War. While food and drugs are essential commodities, air transport is a different story, but from being a kind of luxurious good affordable to a small group of customers, civil aviation has expanded and become accessible to many people around the globe. Also, air transport long ago surpassed passenger ships as a means of transportation,[28] and Figure 3.1 shows this rapid increase over the recent decades.

Attention to the passengers of airline companies, again another word for consumers, was a *sine qua non* for ICAO. The organization made several references to passengers in its constitution, which was included in the Convention on International Civil Aviation,[29] although the sovereignty of states and competition were the major themes – and still are. To foster "equality of opportunity," as mentioned in the preamble of the Convention, has always been an official goal, and during recent decades privatization has become one of the current measures to boost competition – to the benefit of consumers.

Although cargo is a key component of civil aviation, there is no real and encompassing civil aviation without passengers, and the reputation of airlines very much hinges on meeting their essential demands and expectations. It is consequently in the profound interest of airlines, airports and all other operators in the sector that passengers travel safely, but in the language of aviation, safety also relates to aircraft, crews and many other aspects, although reference to "security" is common when addressing the quality and standards of technical and

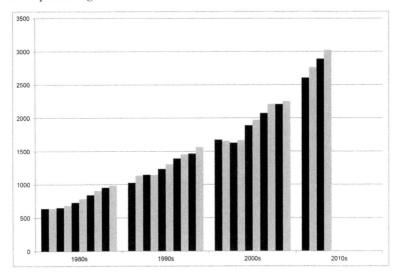

Figure 3.1 Number of airline passengers 1980–2013 (millions)
Source: http://data.worldbank.org/indicator/IS.AIR.PSGR.

organizational facilities in the air and on the ground. From the perspective of governments, it is important that there be fast and reliable forms of transport available to connect societies, and that passengers have an exceptional level of trust in civil aviation. Governments are expected to adopt regulation to guarantee the safety of passengers and to conduct investigations to upgrade safety whenever needed. This includes, for instance, measures to combat terrorism: in 1963 the Tokyo Convention on Offences and Certain Other Acts Committed on Board Aircraft was adopted, and in 1971 the Montreal Convention for the Suppression of Unlawful Acts against the Safety of Civil Aviation was adopted; these conventions have since been amended and followed by other initiatives.[30]

Because much civil aviation is transboundary and, to a large extent, faces similar technical challenges round the world, it is only natural that various forms of regulation are adopted in a global framework, and that experiences are filtered into and evaluated by competent international agencies. However, most of these regulations tend to escape notice by the overwhelming majority of passengers, who do not understand the technical language of aviation and who rely on the joint efforts of airlines and governments to provide the required amount of safety. Only on rare occasions do passengers experience the detrimental effects of rule violations and disasters.

According to the articles and annexes of the Chicago Convention inaugurating the ICAO, the agency develops – in cooperation with other technical bodies and interested parties – thousands of so-called standards and recommended practices (SARPS) to regulate global aviation.[31] For instance, ICAO is involved in the development of the Advance Passenger Information (API) system, which is created primarily to help states develop efficient border controls, but which also harbors some advantages for passengers by making travel and control swifter. In some fields, however, procedures to collect passenger information may interfere with privacy concerns, and thus implementation varies across countries and regions.

Several regulations relate to passengers, and several of the organization's bureaus are active with relevance to passengers, especially the Air Transport Bureau, responsible for safety, but no unit has been established to cater to passengers alone. This indicates that passenger concerns are integrated into many other tasks, but it also shows that consumer interests are not always articulated as such and expressed in the organizational structure of ICAO, and we find no real platform for building ties with civil society organizations, including consumer organizations.[32]

Passengers enjoy certain consumer rights, an issue that has received increasing attention but which is not related only to safety. Some rules are national or regional, but we also find global measures. The most explicit rules to protect consumers are formulated primarily in the Warsaw Convention,[33] adopted in 1929 in the early days of international civil aviation, amended through the Hague Protocol in 1955 and further revisions, and for most countries replaced by the Montreal Convention, which was signed in 1999 and entered into force in 2003.

Some rules of the old Warsaw Convention, and also in the current Montreal Convention, may seem rather self-evident. A number of the articles relate to the rights of passengers before, during and after flights. They imply, for instance, the duty of airlines to provide correct and timely information on the departure and destination of travel, and they also address the tagging of baggage. More controversially the convention "governs and may limit the liability of carriers in respect of death or injury and for destruction or loss of, or damage to, baggage, and for delay."[34] Also other clauses in the convention regulate these critical issues of death and injury of passengers, as well as damage to and delayed baggage. These various articles on compensation in case of death and injury of passengers, the liability of the carriers regarding loss of baggage and delay, and the complaints rights of passengers are crucial to consumer protection in air transport. Because passengers are responsible for their own behavior and for taking care of their own baggage, carriers cannot always be held responsible for negligence and loss, and the convention text addresses these problems and specifies how to evaluate the different conditions and liability provisions. However, it is clear that over time, consumer issues have received greater attention in the convention and in the work of the ICAO more generally. More rights have been granted to passengers, and compensation and liability levels have increased, but consumer and industry interests are not always easy to align, and different regulatory traditions prevail throughout the world.[35] However, in August 2014 the ICAO Air Transport Regulatory Panel agreed on a draft text stipulating core principles on consumer protection,[36] an issue that had already been dealt with in the context of the airline companies the year before.

We stated in this section on ICAO that the organization is more or less alone, at least in the core field of global aviation policy, including different issues pertaining to consumers, but this is correct only insofar as other intergovernmental organizations are concerned. ICAO entertains strong relations with business, a very important partner being the International Aviation Transport Association (IATA), which is also heavily involved in rule-making. Much knowledge is shared between the organizations that, in many ways, form the pillars of a special knowledge community. We return to this organization and its role in consumer policy in Chapter 5.

ITU: consumer policy subordinate to competition policy

Although in the past the command of telecommunications was often associated with national security, and in many respects still is, we cannot reduce telecommunications to this field of politics alone. Today much policy-making in telecommunications has to do with the regulation of business, and in some areas even with the protection of consumers, but the linkages between consumer policy and telecommunications are only modestly covered in research. However, in the different international organizations involved in telecommunications, it is at least common to allude to consumers, or occasionally end-users, irrespective of the goods and services purchased, making the distinct roles of buyers and sellers instantly recognizable. In some areas governments play a significant role as part of public service commitments, but in other areas the private sector is dominant, in some cases as the result of privatization and globalization, and consumers must search for information and choose between competing firms in the market.

At the global level, the principal role is played by the International Telecommunication Union (ITU), which develops strategies and adopts various kinds of rules to regulate the sector, also with a view to improving the quality of products and services and protecting consumers. The ITU can trace its roots back to the early formation of international organizations in the nineteenth century,[37] but the agency has since been amalgamated with other organizations and reformed to accommodate different areas of telecommunications and to embrace a plethora of innovative technologies and products entering an expanding and complex market. Ever since the introduction of telegraph, radio, telephone, television and now the internet, information and communication technologies have undergone dynamic developments through which a diversity of products and services are made available to consumers, and without which many areas of modern societies would not function.

Unlike some other intergovernmental organizations engaged in specific areas of consumer policy (such as WHO and FAO, which have specialized consumer departments built into their structure, signaling an official commitment to consumer protection), the ITU does not have any particular entities that cater to consumer concerns. This does not suggest, however, that consumer issues are ignored, but they are standing somewhat in the background.

A large number of study groups and other bodies are tasked with the formulation and recommendation of standards for the ITU to approve, and standard setting is the key form of regulation in the organization. These bodies are open to ITU members and external actors, but consumers have only weak participation compared with the participation of the private sector. Consumer groups do not dispose of the same degree of expert knowledge to deliver strong input into these processes. In the study groups, typically operating in study cycles, the private sector has more intimate relations with the ITU, and business participates at strategic policy levels in the Global Industry Leaders Forum (GILF) and in the Global Regulators–Industry Dialogue (GRID). Equivalent forums to consult with the consumer movement are not available, however.

It can be difficult to understand what is behind the technical language of the large number of standards and how they affect consumers, but if global standards are agreed upon, then consumers in principle gain access to a rich variety of products whose operability is guaranteed in different parts of the world. As with many other agencies involved in the formulation of general consumer strategies, and dealt with in Chapter 2, a basic tenet of the ITU is to enhance competition.

According to the ITU philosophy, "international ICT standards avoid costly market battles over preferred technologies, and for companies from emerging markets, they create a level playing field which provides access to new markets. They are an essential aid to developing countries in building their infrastructure and encouraging economic development, and through economies of scale, they can reduce costs for all: manufacturers, operators and consumers."[38] This kind of rule-making very much applies the language of competition policy, but certain efforts of the ITU are expressed in terms of consumer policy.

Occasionally the ITU has sponsored research to examine the integration of consumer concerns in the sector. In 2002 one of these reports concluded that "worldwide, consumer protection issues in telecommunications services are generally not given full consideration."[39] Although major failures were identified at national levels, particularly in developing countries, stronger international efforts were also due.

A step forward was taken in 2010 at the World Telecommunication Development Conference, an ITU event, with the passing of Resolution 64 which instructed the ITU to improve the position of consumers within a broad range of areas.[40] The conference also formulated a number of guidelines and recommendations, and mentioned the efforts taken by other organizations, such as the UN, OECD and ISO, which in some areas are more experienced in combining consumer protection, standard setting and internet regulation.

Following these initiatives, the recent World Telecommunication Development Conference in Dubai decided to launch a new study to further examine the deficiencies in national, regional and international regulation, and to formulate proposals that bridge the gap between the rapid development of technology and the comparatively slow development in related consumer protection. A long list of issues is tabled for investigation and discussion with a view to submitting a final report in 2017.[41]

It seems that a more systematic effort is being prepared to strengthen consumer protection and move beyond the considerations for consumer concerns filtered into the existing work on standard setting. While there are clear barriers to the integration of consumer concerns, consumer protection in the sector is addressed by other organizations, indicating that the ITU as an intergovernmental agency has not quite managed to keep its position as the most relevant forum for global policy-making in all areas of information and communication technologies. As we have seen in Chapter 2, the OECD plays an active role in internet politics.

Furthermore, new bodies emerge to solve problems in public policy that have been associated mainly with governments and intergovernmental organizations, and thus reflect a broader trend in global governance to establish bodies based on other principles of cooperation. The Internet Corporation for Assigned Names and Numbers (ICANN) is a private, US-based entity under contract to the US government, and has emerged as the primary organization to regulate the internet. Born in a different age from the old ITU, ICANN is fashioned as a bottom-up organization open to stakeholder engagement and input from many different knowledge holders, and there is even consumer participation under the "Non-Commercial Users Constituency,"[42] as it is called, but of course consumers are confronted with basic problems of mobilizing and sustaining resources. Consumer choice and consumer trust are parts of its accountability and transparency program, and some of these concerns are filtered into regulation.

UNWTO: consumer interests combined with other concerns

The final intergovernmental organization studied in this chapter is the World Tourism Organization (UNWTO). Founded as a private organization, it was transformed into an intergovernmental organization and finally became a UN agency in 2003.[43] In part, this relocation from the private to the public sector reflects the rapid development of tourism as a global industry and the demand for organizing global policies around it, giving the industry a more prominent platform, and giving the UN an opportunity to embrace this important policy field.

The UNWTO mitigates various kinds of conflicts, and to different degrees draws the interested parties, including both tourism industry and tourists, into its work. The tourism industry is very diverse, however, and there are many types of tourist: people purchasing package tours, passengers on cruise ships, event travelers, airline passengers, among others.[44] Tourists are officially recognized as constituting an important interest and may be referred to as both tourists and consumers.[45] Although there is a key emphasis on competition in the organization, the role of tourists is also seen in a broader context of consumer policy, therefore tourists face some of the same challenges as consumers in other markets. No special entities, such as departments or committees, are created to cater exclusively to consumer problems. The industry, however, has strong links with the UNWTO.[46]

As market actors engaging with different branches of the tourism industry, tourists, like other consumers, need various forms of consumer protection. Much regulation related to tourists is adopted at regional and national levels, but the UNWTO is actively involved in the formulation of global policies.[47] A basic issue is tourism safety and security, an area that has claimed the attention of the organization since the late 1980s, and has led to the adoption of various recommendations and the issuing of manuals to assist tour operators to ameliorate these measures.[48] Today these efforts have been expanded in different directions, and recommendations and guidelines include everything from the prevention of diseases to the management of disasters and the avoidance of organized crime and terrorism, all harmful to tourists. Today these activities are built into the encompassing UNWTO Risk and Crisis Management Program, implementation of which is supported by the secretariat.

Before the organization became recognized as a UN special agency, it adopted the Global Code of Ethics for Tourism (GCET) in 1999,[49] which was then dealt with by ECOSOC and recognized by the UN General Assembly through a special resolution in 2001, reiterating the importance of tourism and the role of consumer protection in tourism. The code covered different issues in global tourism and contained various recommendations on consumer protection, although this was not the central element in the code. Apparently, this kind of soft regulation was not sufficient to advance the rights of consumers. Today implementation of the code is monitored by the World Committee on Tourism Ethics (WCTE), one of the organization's committees, which has welcomed new initiatives in consumer protection, needed to realize some of the goals expressed in the code.

An important step to augment consumer protection was taken in 2010 when the UNWTO recognized that "the sector is facing an insufficiency of global binding rules governing the rights and responsibilities of tourists/consumers and tour operators."[50] Accordingly, a working group was tasked with drafting a proposal that could eventually lead to the adoption of an international convention to protect consumers, and with the help of the UNWTO secretariat further studies and discussions have been carried out. Starting out with a focus on *force majeure* problems, the work has been extended to cover multiple dimensions of consumer protection, including various contractual and informational problems in the agreements between business and consumers. Work on conventions in intergovernmental organizations usually takes many years to complete, and so far a draft text with annexes has been developed detailing those areas where binding rules should be applied,[51] and fields where recommendations are preferred. A draft is currently circulating but no final proposal for a convention has been prepared, and there is also doubt among some business associations as to whether a convention is actually needed and helpful to business. It is interesting to note that a long list of business associations from different branches of the tourism industry are mentioned as participants in the working group, whereas there is no trace of consumer representatives. Such a convention would be much more powerful than the soft measures of codes, guidelines and recommendations that encourage business to adopt higher standards and upgrade consumer protection but allow segments of the industry to ignore regulation.

As part of the globalization process, tourism is today very diverse and brings together people from different parts of the world, but there is still a bias – most tourists come from the Global North, and in the meeting between different cultures and income levels there exists a potential conflict. However, in many countries tourism is the primary source of revenue, so there are many benefits for developing countries in increasing the number of tourists, and yet there are clear problems associated with the risk of destroying fragile habitats and social traditions.

To enable a form of tourism that is sustainable in economic, social and environmental terms, new demands are placed on the industry and on travelers to behave responsibly, and the UNWTO has formulated relevant policies to address the negative and positive externalities of modern tourism. Such policies combine consumer policy with other policies, and cannot pay attention solely to the interests of consumers, as this would probably stimulate excessive consumerism. Of particular importance is development policy, and links are forged with other organizations to meet the Millennium Development Goals defined by the UN;[52] environmental policy and climate policy are also addressed and require coordination with other intergovernmental organizations.

This is another illustration of the fact that intergovernmental organizations working in special areas of consumer policies, just like the general organizations defining broader strategies and principles, are sometimes challenged to work together with other organizations holding the same or different kinds of expertise. This issue is dealt with in Chapter 4 on inter-agency coordination.

Conclusion

Because of comparatively specific mandates, some organizations are involved in areas of consumer policy relevant only to certain industries and certain consumer segments or needs. As a rule, these issues are not covered by the general organizations analyzed in Chapter 2, but are the clear and undisputed domain of each of the special organizations. Although principles, guidelines and recommendations can definitely be found here as well, policies tend to have a more concrete and binding character, but still require efforts at domestic levels to implement strategies, involving public and private actors alike. This chapter has focused on agencies with rather substantial engagement in consumer protection and cooperation with business and consumers, but despite the clear variation that exists between them, it is possible to summarize the major and common features of their work.

First, each of the special organizations typically regulates areas pertaining to a single industry, or a group of related industries, and a variety of associated consumer issues. Global regulation is essential to the working of these industries (pharmaceuticals, food, airlines, travel agencies, telecommunications) characterized by global firms and transboundary operations, and these organizations strongly attract the attention of the regulated industries. Emphasizing the role of competition, there is considerable interest within business to establish a level playing field and to demonstrate responsible behavior to regulators and specific subsets of consumers, but this kind of targeted regulation also offers consumers an opportunity to oversee and hold specific industries accountable rather than discuss broader principles.

Second, consumer-related activities in special organizations are in most cases characterized by a chain of related initiatives rather than isolated efforts, and the agencies advance consumer protection at a rather detailed level. These activities are further displaying a strong continuity: several of the organizations reviewed here have a relatively long and uninterrupted record of engagement in consumer protection and in defending their domains. This long-time commitment includes regular updating of core pieces of regulation, but the firm tradition also allows for the inclusion of new issues in their overall consumer strategies.

Third, a common feature is the overall importance of expert knowledge in running these organizations, and this also applies to their activities in consumer policy, where certain types of professional expertise are essential and bring the organizations and interested parties together. This is particularly vivid in matters relating to safety and the basic physical protection of consumers, almost iconic for consumer policy, and this capacity is central in the work of organizations such as FAO, ICAO and WHO, but also has a role to play in the ITU and UNWTO, where other kinds of knowledge are demanded.

When regulation is targeted at particular sectors of the economy, the special organizations examined in this chapter must build their work on related knowledge. In the special agencies working with different issues of consumer protection, knowledge is closely associated with different areas of business, thus the industry knowledge and professional knowledge needed to formulate and implement policies may overlap in many cases. This problem is not scrutinized in research on knowledge communities, but this composite knowledge may privilege business in many ways. Additional studies of food, health, transport and tourism policies are required to analyze the different forms of knowledge filtered into the special organizations and into consumer protection.

Organizations with broad tasks in consumer policy usually address issues of a rather general nature and rarely go into specific areas. Other intergovernmental organizations, each assigned a small subfield of consumer policy, and practically unchallenged by other agencies, tend to concentrate on yet another group of issues. However, if we do not study the role of inter-agency coordination, then we are not able to offer a full analysis of global consumer organizations. Many different forms of cooperation exist between organizations and are necessitated by the complex and dynamic character of global consumer policy. This is the theme of Chapter 4.

Notes

1 Different categorizations of intergovernmental organizations are referenced in the scholarly literature: Volker Rittberger, Bernhard Zangl and Andreas Kruck, *International Organization*, 2nd edn (Houndmills: Palgrave, 2012); Margaret P. Karns and Karen A. Mingst, *International Organizations: The Politics and Processes of Global Governance*, 2nd edn (Boulder, Colo.: Lynne Rienner, 2009). The UN – and its subsidiary bodies – is seen as the general organization, in principle being responsible for all intergovernmental cooperation, whereas the specialized agencies work independently according to their own constitutions. This understanding is useful for analyzing the hierarchies, or lack of them, but not how public policies, in our case consumer policy, are organized at the global level.

2 WHO, *Twelfth General Programme of Work. Not Merely the Absence of Disease* (Geneva: World Health Organization, 2014). Nitsan Chorev, *The World Health Organization between North and South* (Ithaca, NY: Cornell University Press, 2012).

3 The WHO constitution broadly refers to "people." WHO, *Constitution of the World Health Organization*, 45th edn, supplement (Geneva: World Health Organization, 2006).

4 Many WHO activities relate to the pharmaceutical industry, but some initiatives have other targets, such as the baby food industry (International Code of Marketing of Breast Milk Substitutes, adopted by WHO in 1981) and the tobacco industry (WHO Framework Convention on Tobacco Control, adopted by WHO in 2003). Kelley Lee, *The World Health Organization (WHO)* (London: Routledge, 2009), 87–95.

5 A basic issue is access to and quality of medicines. This issue is addressed by the Interagency Pharmaceutical Coordination group (IPC) established in 1996.

6   WHO, *Rational Use of Medicines: Activities*, see www.who.int/medicines/a reas/rational_use/rud_activities/en.

7   WHO, *Guidelines on Developing Consumer Information on Proper Use of Traditional, Complementary and Alternative Medicine* (Geneva: World Health Organization, 2004). This has been followed up by other guidelines on safety monitoring.

8   WHO, *Guidelines on Developing Consumer Information on Proper Use of Traditional, Complementary and Alternative Medicine* (Geneva: World Health Organization, 2004), section 1.2: 5.

9   WHO, "Good Practices in the Manufacture and Quality Control of Drugs (resolution WHA22.50)," in *Twenty-second World Health Assembly, Boston, Massachusetts, 8–25 July 1969. Part 1: Resolutions and Decisions, Annexes* (Geneva: World Health Organization, 1969), 99–105 (Official Records of the World Health Organization No. 176).

10 The Convention for the Mutual Recognition of Inspection in Respect of the Manufacture of Pharmaceutical Products was adopted in 1970, but today two arrangements work in parallel, the Pharmaceutical Inspection Convention (PIC) and the Pharmaceutical Inspection Co-operation Scheme (PIC Scheme), and were reorganized in 2014. They include only the developed industrialized countries, however. www.picscheme.org/pics.php.

11 WHO, *Ethical Criteria for Medicinal Drug Promotion*. World Health Organization Resolution WHA41.17 adopted by the Forty-first World Health Assembly (Geneva: World Health Organization, 1988).

12 Ibid., 1.

13 Editorial, "CIOMS/WHO meeting on ethical criteria for medicinal drug promotion," *Essential Drugs Monitor* 17 (1994): 18.

14 Pauline Norris, Andrew Herxheimer, Joel Lexchin and Peter Mansfield, *Drug Promotion. What we Know, What we Have yet to Learn. Reviews of Materials in the WHO/HAI Database on Drug Promotion* (Geneva and Amsterdam: World Health Organization and Health Action International, 2005).

15 There is a voluminous body of literature discussing the role of the pharmaceutical industry and the risks of capturing governments and international agencies. Pauline Norris, Andrew Herxheimer, Joel Lexchin and Peter Mansfield, *Drug Promotion: What We Know, What We Have Yet to Learn* (Geneva: World Health Organization/Health Action International, 2005); M.N.G. Dukes, *The Law and Ethics of the Pharmaceutical Industry* (Amsterdam: Elsevier, 2006); Sara E. Davies, *Global Politics of Health* (Cambridge: Polity, 2010), Chapter 7; Susan K. Sell, "TRIPS: Fifteen Years Later," *Journal of Intellectual Property Law* 18, no. 2 (2014). Date Posted: 1 August 2011. Last Revised: 25 May 2014.

16 WHO, *Counterfeit Drugs. Guidelines for the Development of Measures to Combat Counterfeit Drugs* (Geneva: World Health Organization, 1999).

17 Safety is also related to efforts to avoid the spread of diseases, and thus affects international trade and travel. This challenge is addressed in the International Health Regulations (IHR) of the WHO revised in 2005. David P. Fidler, "From international sanitary conventions to global health security: the new international health regulations," *Chinese Journal of International Law* 4, no. 2 (2005): 325–92.

18 Different regulatory systems are important in the governance of policy fields and are analyzed in comparative studies: David Vogel, *The Politics of*

Precaution. Regulating Health, Safety and Environmental Risks in Europe and the United States (Princeton, N.J.: Princeton University Press, 2012).

19 FAO, *Guidelines for Ensuring Balanced Representation of Civil Society in FAO Meetings and Processes* (Rome: Food and Agriculture Organization, n.d.); FAO, *Principles and Guidelines for FAO Cooperation with the Private Sector* (Rome: Food and Agriculture Organization, 2000). The *FAO Policy Concerning Relations with International Non-governmental Organizations* goes back to the early days of the organization, see: www.fao.org/docrep/x5576e/x5576e0i.htm.

20 Food security is part of the broader security agenda, but consumer dimension is less prevalent here. David Fullbrook, "Food as security," *Food Security* 2, no. 1 (2010): 5–20; Bryan L. McDonald, *Food Security* (Cambridge: Polity Press, 2010). However, if we see food security in a North–South perspective, it is clear that security has significant implications for Southern consumers: Jennifer Clapp, *Food* (Cambridge: Polity Press, 2012).

21 The Committee on World Food Security (CFS) was formed in 1974 and significantly reformed in 2009. CFS, *Global Strategic Framework for Food Security & Nutrition* (Rome: Committee on World Food Security, 2013).

22 FAO, "New paradigm: Quality," press release, January 2006. www.fao.org/ag/magazine/pdf/0601-1.pdf. Somewhat confusingly the website refers to six departments but lists only five: www.fao.org/about/who-we-are/departments/en.

23 FAO, "Meat quality," www.fao.org/ag/againfo/themes/en/meat/quality_meat.html.

24 For some of the principles guiding this strategy, see FAO, *Specific Quality and Voluntary Standards* (Rome: Food and Agriculture Organization, n.d.).

25 For a good overview of the different public and private efforts, Renata Clarke, "Private food safety standards: their role in food safety regulation and their impact," paper prepared for the 33rd Session of the Codex Alimentarius Commission (Rome: Food and Agriculture Organization, 2010).

26 F.K. Käferstein, Y. Motarjemi and D.W. Bettcher, "December foodborne disease control: a transnational challenge," *Emerging Infectious Diseases* 3, no. 4 (1997): 503–10; Diane G. Newell, Marion Koopmans, Linda Verhoef, Erwin Duizer, Awa Aidara-Kane, Hein Sprong, Marieke Opsteegh, Merel Langelaar, John Threfall, Flemming Scheutz, Joke van der Giessen and Hilde Kruse, "Food-borne diseases – the challenges of 20 years ago still persist while new ones continue to emerge," *International Journal of Food Microbiology* 139 (2010): S3–S15.

27 Maybe somewhat surprisingly, the International Atomic Energy Agency (IAEA) is involved in detecting chemicals in food using various nuclear techniques.

28 In the maritime sector, the role of passenger ships has declined, but regulations to ensure the safety of passengers, some of which were introduced decades ago, as mentioned in Chapter 1, are still in force. Today these are particularly important for cruise ships, a booming area of sea transport, and here a key role is assumed by the International Maritime Organization (IMO). In particular, see IMO, *International Convention for the Safety of Life at Sea (SOLAS)* (London: International Maritime Organization, 2011).

29 ICAO, *Convention on Civil Aviation* ("Chicago Convention"), 7 December 1944, 15 U.N.T.S. 295, www.refworld.org/docid/3ddca0dd4.html.

30 ICAO, *Convention on Offences and Certain Other Acts Committed on Board Aircraft*, Tokyo, 14 September 1963; ICAO, Convention for the *Suppression of Unlawful Acts against Safety of Civil Aviation*, Montreal, 23 September 1971.

31 Many standards are adopted by general bodies such as ISO and also applied to different sectors, but in air traffic ICAO is responsible for this detailed and highly specific work. ICAO, *Making an ICAO Standard*, www. icao.int/safety/airnavigation/Pages/standard.aspx.

32 When, for instance, effectiveness was discussed in ICAO in the late 1990s, only industry was mentioned under external relations. See www.icao.int/ Meetings/AMC/MA/Assembly%2032nd%20Session/069.pdf.

33 ICAO, *Convention for the Unification of Certain Rules Relating to International Carriage by Air*, Warsaw 12 October 1929.

34 ICAO, *Convention for the Unification of Certain Rules for International Carriage by Air* (Montreal, 28 May 1999), Chapter II – "Documentation and Duties of the Parties Relating to the Carriage of Passengers, Baggage and Cargo," article 3, paragraph 4.

35 Ken Button, *The Impacts of Globalisation on International Air Transport Activity. Past Trends and Future Perspectives* (Paris: OECD/International Transport Forum, 2008); Bin Cheng, "A new era in the law of international carriage by air: from Warsaw (1929) to Montreal (1999)," *International and Comparative Law Quarterly* 53, no. 4 (2004): 833–59; Tory A. Weigand, "Recent developments under the Montreal Convention," *Defense Counsel Journal* 77, no. 4 (2010).

36 ICAO, *ICAO Air Transport Regulatory Panel Agrees Core Principles on Consumer Protection*, 22 August 2014. http://airlines.iata.org/agenda/icao-a ir-transport-regulatory-panel-agrees-core-principles-on-consumer-protection.

37 Bob Reinalda, *Routledge History of International Organizations: From 1815 to the Present Day* (London: Routledge, 2009), 92–3.

38 ITU-T in Brief. See www.itu.int/en/ITU-T/about/Pages/default.aspx.

39 Geoffrey Cannock, *Feedback to Regulators from Consumers. Apoyo Consultoria Report to the International Telecommunication Union (ITU)*. Global Symposium for Regulators, 7–8 December 2002, Hong Kong, China (Geneva: International Telecommunication Union, 2002). See also ITU, *Consumer Protection in the Digital Age: Assessing Current and Future Activities*. Document: 3. Global Seminar on Quality of Service and Consumer Protection, 31 August–1 September 2006 (Geneva: International Telecommunication Union, 2006).

40 ITU, *Question 18–2/1: Enforcing National Policies and Regulations on Consumer Protection Notably in a Converging Environment* (Geneva: International Telecommunication Union, 2014).

41 ITU, *Question 6/1: Consumer Information, Protection and Rights: Laws, Regulation, Economic Bases, Consumer Networks* (Geneva: International Telecommunication Union, 2014).

42 ICANN, *Bylaws for Internet Corporation for Assigned Names and Numbers*, as amended 7 February 2014.

43 J. Jafari, "Creation of the Intergovernmental World Tourism Organization," *Annals of Tourism Research* 2, no. 5 (1974): 237–45. This analysis

traces the organization's early development, but major changes in its status were accomplished just before and after the turn of the millennium.

44 Neil Leiper, "Why 'the tourism industry' is misleading as a generic expression: the case for the plural variation, 'tourism industries'," *Tourism Management* 29, no. 2 (2008): 237–51.

45 As early as 1963, the United Nations Conference on Tourism and International Travel tried to define these categories and referred to both "tourists" and "visitors." Nell Leiper, "The framework of tourism: towards a definition of tourism, tourist, and the tourist industry," *Annals of Tourism Research* 6, no. 4 (1979): 390–407; Frédéric Darbellay and Mathis Stock, "Tourism as complex interdisciplinary research object," *Annals of Tourism Research* 39, no. 1 (2012): 441–58. The international dimension of regulation is not given priority but should be added to understand this area of consumer policy.

46 Interestingly, UNWTO is not a pure intergovernmental organization with only states as members. UNWTO also has affiliate members, which are typically drawn from different parts of the tourism industry, and there is a significant number of them. Today they are organized through the group of affiliate members, but in the past there also existed a UNWTO Business Council for this part of the membership. www2.unwto.org/content/pa nelists-biographies. Karsten Ronit, "Transnational corporations and the regulation of business at the global level," in *The Ashgate Research Companion to Non-State Actors*, ed. Bob Reinalda (Farnham: Ashgate, 2011), 75–87.

47 David L. Edgell Sr and Jason Swanson, *Tourism Policy and Planning: Yesterday, Today, and Tomorrow*, 2nd edn (London: Routledge, 2013).

48 WTO, *Tourism Safety and Security: Practical Measures for Destinations* (Madrid: World Tourism Organization, 1996).

49 UNWTO, *Global Code of Ethics for Tourism* (Madrid: World Tourism Organization, 1999).

50 UNWTO, *Workshop on the Protection of Tourists/Consumers and Travel Organizers*, www2.unwto.org/event/workshop-protection-touristsconsumers-a nd-travel-organizers.

51 UNWTO, *Update on the Draft UNWTO Convention on the Protection of Tourists and Tourism Service Providers: Note by the Secretary-General*. CAP/CSA/25/5.5_Protection (Madrid: World Tourism Organization, 2013).

52 Martin Mowforth and Ian Munt, *Tourism and Sustainability: Development, Globalisation and New Tourism in the Third World*, 3rd edn (London: Routledge, 2009).

4 Coordination between agencies and across issues

- Coordination – between development, trade, competition and consumer policies
- Coordination – between education, development and consumer policies
- Coordination – between trade, competition and consumer policies
- Coordination – between sustainability, development and consumer policies
- Coordination – between food, health and consumer policies
- Conclusion

There is no overarching global body responsible for consumer policy and capable of picking up new challenges, but a range of activities are carried out single-handedly by intergovernmental organizations, both by those that seek to define general rules and guidelines in consumer policy and by those committed to special areas. However, many issues cross different institutional boundaries, and new organizational formats must be created to host such issues. Here inter-agency coordination becomes relevant and warrants an additional analysis. We have briefly discussed certain aspects of cooperation, but have retained some well established cases of coordination for further scrutiny in this chapter.

Several organizations are involved in inter-agency coordination. Some have an *ad hoc* character and are soon dissolved, while other activities are taken care of within a permanent institutional framework where resources are pooled and principles of cooperation are formally agreed. This is a recognition that single agencies are not always competent to effectively administer a given field of consumer policy or influential enough to provide the sufficient amount of legitimacy.

Still, there are many options in inter-agency coordination. Should a smaller or larger group of bodies be drawn into cooperation? Will general and special organizations be required to solve the task? Can affected interests among consumers and business be properly integrated in problem-solving? These are some of the questions to be posed when coordination is required, but there is no blueprint for coordination, and a variety of combinations attest to the great flexibility of arrangements.

In inter-agency work, different traditions, interests and approaches are brought together, and in this process the existing domains of the participating organizations are tested. This is a particular challenge when the mandates of the agencies are expanding and when ambitions to move into new areas are fostered, leading to adaptations in organizational structures and strategies. The challenges to existing turfs are a perennial issue in theories of bureaucratic politics, but these are not sufficiently developed for analyzing the different problems of inter-governmental bodies. However, this chapter offers some clues as to how these can be studied.

Although coordination is essentially based on the joint interests of participating agencies, the many actors have different knowledge bases and offer different solutions. The agencies involved do not always play the same role in coordination. Often one organization assumes the lead role and provides the core facilities, thus some kind of hierarchy may exist between the agencies, but it is also important that a consensus be achieved and that the contributions of different agencies be recognized.

There are a number of policy clusters that cross multiple agencies, necessitating coordination and leading to the creation of new bodies, but that are still tied to existing organizations. In this chapter we focus on some of the major interfaces and institutions created to facilitate coordination: First, a few organizations are engaged in defining the overall principles in global consumer policy, and agencies such as ECOSOC, UNCTAD and the OECD are called to address this challenge, but departing from the UN Guidelines for Consumer Protection coordination has in recent years centered on the issue of development. Second, a special element in the Guidelines, but having its own agendas and its own coordinating mechanisms, is consumer education. Different strategies are elaborated by agencies, such as UNESCO and the OECD, to enhance the competencies of consumers, and recent advancements have been made with regard to financial literacy. Third, we witness interesting developments within trade, where the WTO interacts with other bodies and links competition, trade and consumer policies. Although traditional emphasis is placed on competition and barriers to trade, consumer protection is addressed in many areas of standard setting. Fourth, sustainability has become a hot issue over recent decades and it embraces the patterns of modern production and consumption, giving rise to coordination between different agencies to formulate and implement new strategies. Fifth, classical consumer issues relate to nutrition, link health and food policy, and demand coordination between FAO and WHO, where separate bodies exist to manage coordination in all areas of food safety.

Coordination – between development, trade, competition and consumer policies

We saw that UNCTAD as a prolific trade and development organization is engaged in global consumer policy, most of the time in a general fashion without taking specific notice of particular industries and commodities. This endeavor includes some degree of coordination with other agencies, and it gives coordination a certain twist as development in third world countries is the overriding concern of UNCTAD. Hence a blend of trade, development, competition and consumer policies emerges in the coordination of strategies. Many agencies can potentially become involved, suggesting that conflicts over general approaches and concrete priorities will surface. In reality, few organizations can be seen as key players, but they all have distinct commitments and strategies.

In recent years, coordination with other organizations has become an essential requirement with regard to the UN Guidelines for Consumer Protection, adopted in 1985. When UNCTAD was tasked in 2000 with reviewing the UN Guidelines for Consumer Protection, as part of the process to combat restrictive business practices initiated in the 1970s and early 1980s,[1] so-called expert meetings on consumer interests, competition and development, as they were first called, were arranged by UNCTAD. In this way the organization somehow took over the administration of the guidelines, which span a rich variety of subjects. In the following years the guidelines became the central concern for the agency in the area of consumer policy and received continuous attention through different series of meetings. It took time, however, to adopt new plans and move toward a revision. Further concrete steps were taken in 2010–12 to discuss implementation of the guidelines and revise them, a process in which the International Advisory Group of Experts on Consumer Protection assists UNCTAD. This process is still not finished.

Although these tasks were still closely related to the annual review conferences on restrictive business practices, an old issue in the organization, UNCTAD embarked on a new and broader mission in global consumer policy. The guidelines are supposed to further the consumer cause across the world and assist all governments to implement the principles. Notwithstanding these general ambitions, it was acknowledged at the same time that there were particularly strong demands for improvements in consumer protection in countries with inadequate institutional capacity and limited domestic consumer protection in place, and that amendments should account for these challenges.[2]

Therefore the current revision of the guidelines necessitates coordination with other agencies to gather experiences and ultimately pave the way for updating, but the process of revision also requires coordination to improve strategies, particularly in developing countries. Part of the mandate to revise the guidelines was therefore to "formulate appropriate recommendations for action in capacity-building as well as international cooperation in this field."[3] The papers prepared by the UNCTAD secretariat and the expert meetings deliberating possible revisions have a general orientation at the same time as they highlight North–South inequalities and the special conditions, including issues on competition, in the developing world.

No new, grand body has been created for this purpose. The organizational structure in UNCTAD underpinning the process is relatively modest. To evade the dominance of competition-policy approaches, the work is now organized through separate *ad hoc* expert meetings on consumer protection under UNCTAD's Intergovernmental Group of Experts on Competition Law and Policy, and working groups have been added to examine various aspects.

There are strong contacts with the member states in adjusting the guidelines, offering the states ample opportunities to bring in their national experiences,[4] and we further find certain business and consumer organizations engaged. This reiterates UNCTAD's tradition of exchanging with major non-governmental organizations, including CI and ICC, but it also shows the strategic importance of including the consumer movement in revision of the guidelines. Also, in the past consumer groups played a central role in defining the criteria for consumer protection and in adopting the guidelines. Coordination with other intergovernmental organizations, however, seems to be fairly limited, but other guidelines from the OECD, Organization of American States (OAS), ICPEN, UNCITRAL and CI were mentioned in the secretariats' study on implementation of the UN guidelines. However, only very few other intergovernmental organizations are drawn deeply into this process, and only the OECD takes part in the meetings.

The active participation of the OECD indicates that the guidelines and their revision are not important just from the standpoint of development, but are also of significant interest for the OECD countries where consumer protection is comparatively advanced. It is of course a way of securing influence for the OECD, where there are strong links between competition policy and consumer policy. From the perspective of UNCTAD, the OECD can also serve as an inspiration, and "during the discussions, several areas were identified for incorporation into any future revisions, particularly those where substantive progress has been made in other organizations, such as the OECD."[5] Thus there is an element of policy diffusion.

It is strange that no other organizations are involved on a more solid and permanent basis, given the fact that many agencies today entertain general consumer strategies and have a diversity of institutional interests to defend in consumer policy. It is also noteworthy that agencies such as the United Nations Industrial Development Organization (UNIDO), the United Nations Children's Fund (UNICEF), UNESCO and the World Bank are absent from these meetings, as they have a background in development policy and strong potential to add a development perspective to the coordination of consumer policy.

It is important to bear in mind that, when the original guidelines were drafted in the context of ECOSOC, one of the key organs of the UN, wider coordination was in many ways possible because ECOSOC has some unique commitments and opportunities to coordinate with other bodies according to the UN Charter. UNCTAD is rather a counterweight to the influence of other organizations such as the IMF and WTO.

Right after UNCTAD began to discuss the guidelines in the early 2000s with a revision in mind, a number of other agencies were also involved in this process,[6] including the IMF, UNIDO, WTO and ISO, so coordination has been somewhat fluctuating over the years, although lately with strong contributions from the OECD. Revising the guidelines is a rather specific exercise, but given the encompassing character of the task, it is an exercise with potentially wide-ranging consequences. An active role in inter-agency coordination may not only provide opportunities for influence but also have a symbolic value for the participants, and clearly these different assets are not always exploited.

Many issues – both classic and new – are tabled for negotiations in the revision of the guidelines and invariably link up with different policy areas beyond consumer policy. However, some of these items are discussed outside the framework of UNCTAD and they call for other forms of coordination and involve other combinations of agencies. This applies, for instance, to consumer education.

Coordination – between education, development and consumer policies

To make an informed choice in the market, consumers need reliable information and they also need the skills to evaluate this information. National and international consumer policy refers to "consumer education," a classical item addressed since the early 1960s and an integral part of the UN Guidelines for Consumer Protection. It is therefore given due attention in the revision process discussed above, but coordination is further provided by other organizations and forums.

As UNESCO is the key intergovernmental organization for education, it would be natural for it to assume a leading role and become the anchor organization for consumer education, especially as this applies to developing countries where other demands exist for consumer education. We have also noted some activity in UNESCO, but it is not engaged in coordination in any significant way.[7] UNESCO administers an education project, Teaching and Learning for a Sustainable Future, which is part of the organization's efforts in the area of sustainable lifestyles and a follow-up on the United Nations Commission on Sustainable Development (CSD). There is therefore some coordination with UNEP around concrete projects, but cooperation is at a rather modest level.

Interestingly, the OECD has a higher and differentiated activity in general consumer education,[8] but with a different emphasis stemming from its focus on developed countries, although the organization also compiles data and analyzes the situation in different regions of the world, including Africa. Other agencies seem to find inspiration in the OECD, because consumer protection is relatively advanced in those parts of the world represented by the OECD. However, care is needed when translating these models to other regulatory cultures.

Consumer education is a broad topic, but the principles must also be applied to special issues and industries.[9] Thus particularly interesting developments can be observed within financial education and financial literacy.[10] Especially in the wake of the financial crisis, the question of financial education has attracted much attention. One of the driving forces in the development of programs to generate new skills among consumers is the World Bank. Its report Good Practices for Financial Consumer Protection,[11] published in 2012, envisages new steps in education. This report and ensuing activities harbor an ambition to advance the literacy of consumers in developing countries, and thus perspectives from consumer policy and development policy are brought together. The drafting of the report involved some elements of coordination with other agencies, such as the OECD and the International Network of Financial Services Ombudsman Schemes (Info Network) and the International Financial Consumer Protection Organisation (FinCoNet), and additional input was received from the consumer side through CI. Also, the Alliance for Financial Inclusion (AFI), a group of developing countries, has taken part in the process, and the World Bank was further assisted by the Consultative Group to Assist the Poor (CGAP), housed at the World Bank and involving governments and some international agencies. However, other agencies with distinct development profiles had little if any involvement in this process.

Although the level of consumer education in the OECD member countries is quite different from that in the developing countries, there is still considerable demand for improving the competences of consumers in complex financial markets. Major efforts in financial consumer education were launched in 2002, and issuing several standards, principles and guidelines, the OECD, in some cases in partnership with ISO, became a pioneer in this important niche of consumer policy.

However, the onset of the financial crisis triggered further action and paved the way for coordination relating to financial consumer education and to financial consumer protection more broadly.[12] In such a new policy area, where the roles of the different organizations relevant for coordination are not properly defined, and where different approaches are offered, mutual adaptation is necessary to adopt joint strategies.

In 2008 the OECD International Network on Financial Education (INFE) was established alongside the OECD International Gateway for Financial Education, and according to the OECD "the Gateway is now widely recognized as a global clearinghouse for financial education and awareness, containing information on financial education programs in more than 90 countries."[13] This cooperation involves governments, ministries and private stakeholders, but because participation came from a few global organizations, such as AFI, the World Bank, ILO and IMF,[14] dialogue and coordination could be enhanced.

An important case of inter-agency coordination in financial consumer education has further evolved around the Group of Twenty (G20) and the OECD, and especially after the financial crisis cooperation grew stronger. In 2010, the G20 launched a new initiative,[15] the Global Partnership for Financial Inclusion (GPFI) with three implementing bodies, AFI, CGAP and the International Finance Corporation (IFC). Both the World Bank and the OECD joined later. This initiative embraces G20 countries and non-G20 countries, but there are significant differences in the world with regard to consumer education, as Figure 4.1 shows.

Also in 2010, the G20 encouraged the Financial Stability Board (FSB) to begin further work, together with the OECD plus other relevant organizations including the World Bank, to examine the situation in financial consumer protection, including consumer education. Because the OECD was already highly experienced in the field and was seen as holding the relevant expertise in financial consumer protection and financial consumer education, it was obvious that the OECD should play a leading role in this work together with INFE. The G20/OECD Task Force on Financial Consumer Protection was asked to examine different aspects of consumer protection and provide recommendations to the G20. As a result of this coordination, the G20 countries endorsed the G20 High-Level Principles on Financial Consumer Protection in 2012.[16] It is interesting to note that different interest groups, including consumers through CI, had an opportunity to bring their arguments into the G20, which has some mechanisms to involve civil society organizations.[17]

The project of consumer education is not finished with the adoption of these principles, however. Further guidance is provided to

▇ NS implemented

▇ Advanced state of design of the NS

▓ NS being considered

Figure 4.1 National strategies (NS) for financial education (2013)
Source: OECD, www.oecd.org/finance/financial-education/G20_OECD_NSFinancialEducation.pdf.

governments through the joint recommendations from the OECD and G20 in the area of financial education.[18] In this work the OECD and INFE are playing the leading role, as they host the required expert knowledge and maintain a network to accumulate and evaluate experiences as well as a capacity to disseminate information and recommendations to other international organizations and to governments. This work is relevant not only to the OECD member countries, but also to a wider group of countries that have an ambition to advance consumer education, including in the developing world. In principle, some of these tasks could also be taken on by organizations with a central role in development policy, and we could even expect a greater element of coordination between different agencies than what has been accomplished to date. Consumer education as such is an old field in consumer policy but the institutionalization of new and dynamic areas shows that the division of labor is still not settled.

Coordination – between trade, competition and consumer policies

Trade, competition and consumer policies are intrinsically connected, but international agencies with a strong trade or competition agenda only occasionally make explicit reference to consumer protection. Some agencies, such as the WTO, UNCTAD, ISO and OECD, define consumer policy in a rather general fashion, and with strategies applicable to all sectors, find ways to cooperate with agencies such as FAO and WHO in specific policy areas. It is noteworthy, however, that all these organizations have global commitments and that many trade and consumer issues fall outside their purview. Instead, these issues are approached by regional trade blocs such as the USA and the EU.

Some questions give rise to formal coordination and the creation of new bodies that, to some degree, integrate consumer protection, and do not just treat it as an inevitable by-product of free trade. The primary forum for trade, competition and consumer coordination is the WTO. Many WTO bodies have observers from other agencies, but only a few of them address consumer issues explicitly. It is no surprise that one of the most prolific entities in the WTO combining trade with consumer protection is food-related. An important body linking trade and consumer issues is the Committee on Sanitary and Phytosanitary Measures (SPS Committee), whose mandate is based on the Agreement on the Application of Sanitary and Phytosanitary Measures (SPS Agreement), adopted in 1994 as part of the Uruguay Round agreements, but also building on previous GATT rules, and therefore an essential background for the work of the WTO. The SPS Committee oversees implementation of the agreement, and within this body the Codex Alimentarius Commission, WHO, UNCTAD and ISO, each with its own approach to consumer policy, take part as observers. Thus the committee can be conceived as an institution of inter-agency coordination. While UNCTAD and ISO assist in a general way in the areas of development and standard setting, the Commission, FAO and WHO provide expert knowledge in food safety and health.

The WTO and the committee do not themselves define the standards, a task accomplished by other organizations such as the Codex Alimentarius Commission,[19] whose standards form an important and authoritative background for the committee with regard to food safety, and animal and plant health.[20] Its role will be elaborated further below. Member states should follow the different international standards and guidelines, although different measures can be applied if based on scientific evidence, but they should not be used for the purpose of avoiding competition and protecting domestic producers, and thus be harmful to competition. As such, standards are created with a view to facilitating the conditions of business in international trade. Governments with trained bureaucracies may be better placed to implement rules and to do these investigations,[21] but in a similar vein it can be argued that countries and regions, such as the USA and the EU, with strong bureaucracies, can also defend consumer interests.

The committee is geared toward coordination with other inter-governmental organizations, no mention is made of consumer organizations or other civil society organizations. Many attempts have been made to reform the WTO and make it more open to civil society participation, and changes have been made,[22] but the general tradition of the WTO is not to engage in close consultations with non-governmental organizations. This lack of participation in the committee and limited access to relevant documents have been critically reviewed by consumer organizations,[23] which have to rely on contacts with governments and on better positions in some of the other agencies with a role in standard making and safety matters.

Food safety is an overriding concern in trade policy, and in this sense attention to consumer concerns is key, but consumers are not directly mentioned in the SPS Agreement, although safety is obviously of primary importance to all consumers. The related and general WTO Agreement on Technical Barriers to Trade (TBT) invokes the language of trade and competition policy to a higher degree, and goes more into the protection of consumers in their role as market actors. To some extent this agreement also addresses consumer policy, but no explicit reference is made to consumers either. However, the scope of the agreement and its principles are of value to consumers in many respects.

The Committee on Technical Barriers to Trade, fashioned to take decisions, monitor the agreement and carry out other tasks, can also establish different working groups, and "unnecessary duplication should be avoided between the work under this Agreement and that of governments in other technical bodies."[24] There is definitely an encouragement to coordinate, and the committee also involves a number of other intergovernmental organizations.

In addition to the WTO, coordination efforts can be traced to other major intergovernmental organizations combining trade, competition and consumer policies. UNCTAD and the OECD are active in this field as well. But, as discussed earlier, these organizations define consumer policy on a much broader basis, and not exclusively in relation to trade. There are other forums that in some ways bring together trade, competition and consumer policy on an inter-agency basis, but when we move to these organizations, in some cases the perspective is shifted to competition, with some aspects of trade.

This is the case with the International Competition Network (ICN), which was formed in 2001 as an informal group of competition authorities.[25] It issues a number of recommendations and formulates a variety of best practices. It also attends to consumer concerns and, in its own words, "promotes more efficient and effective antitrust enforcement worldwide to the benefit of consumers and businesses,"[26] but mainly under the headline of competition policy. Apparently this work on competition was not feasible within the existing intergovernmental framework, so a fresh initiative was needed. There is definitely some overlap with other organizations, and mindful of this challenge the ICN is engaged in coordination with the WTO, UNCTAD and OECD, but not with agencies focusing on particular industries. From the perspective of consumer policy, it is important that the ICN strategy should be to consult with consumer representatives, and in this regard the network builds on some of the experiences of the established organizations, such as the OECD and UNCTAD, which have traditions of consumer participation.

Coordination – between sustainability, development and consumer policies

Sustainable consumption was increasingly linked with consumer policy throughout the 1990s, and sustainability was officially added to the UN Guidelines for Consumer Protection in 1999. Evaluations of the guidelines and planned revisions have since then always incorporated the issue of sustainability in their different facets. This also applies to the most recent work on the guidelines carried out under the aegis of UNCTAD, discussed above.

However, sustainability is an issue that trickles down into many policies and organizations, intangible and encompassing at the same time, and we find attempts to bring sustainability and different aspects of consumer policy together in many other forums, leading to fragmentation in the development of policy. There are opportunities to couple sustainability and consumer policy at the general level pertaining to all kinds of production and consumption, and to define strategies valid at the level of particular sectors and, accordingly, devise new coordinating mechanisms to handle these challenges. We therefore have to understand coordination in this new field as quite different from coordination in the more mature institutions discussed in this chapter.

The United Nations Environment Programme (UNEP), which can be seen as the primary organization designated to deal with sustainability policy on a grand scale, is involved in some forms of coordination. An important link is to a familiar theme, and one of the other policy fields discussed in this chapter, namely consumer education. The activities in Education for Sustainable Consumption (ESC) form part of the UN Decade of Education for Sustainable Development (UN DESD, 2005–14), sometimes labelled the Marrakesh Process, and thus embrace many issues other than consumption, but the section on consumption is equally relevant for the Global North and the Global South.

UNEP serves as the secretariat for the sustainable consumption and production dimension in the ten-year program, administers the Global Sustainable Consumption and Production (SCP) Clearinghouse to exchange information, and assists in the implementation of programs. UNEP is further requested to coordinate with a large group of other agencies in areas of sustainable consumption and production.[27] Cooperation is also with selected organizations; there is of course some collaboration with UNESCO, which has led to the adoption of recommendations and guidelines in education for sustainability.[28] UNESCO, on the other hand, has a strong commitment to education, and is the lead agency in the UN Inter-Agency Committee for the Decade on Education for Sustainable Development (IAC-DESD, 2005–14), in which consumer education is one among several other topics.[29]

If we study particular issue areas and segments of consumers, we find UNEP engagement as well. In relation to sustainable tourism, a field characterized by much institutional innovation, UNEP, together with UNWTO and the UN Foundation, takes part in various new bodies created to coordinate initiatives. The Global Sustainable Tourism Council (GSTC) is such an organization, but it would be wrong to see its work only from the perspective of inter-agency coordination, simply because the council involves many interested parties in a multi-stakeholder format, including the tourism industry, a point we return to in Chapter 5. The council also manages the Global Sustainable Tourism Criteria and has adopted a number of standards, some of which combine sustainability with consumer policy.

In some cases, stronger cooperation seems to have evolved among different private parties, including the business community, for instance via the UNEP Forum. First and foremost the marketing and communication industry is engaged in this cooperation: "UNEP intends to involve representatives of the sector from all parts of the world. Advertisers, advertising agencies, media and relevant associations are invited to provide their experience and support, exchange information and co-operate to promote sustainable consumption."[30]

One of the remedies to upgrade consumer protection and flag sustainability is to improve information from companies and offer consumers informed choices. Appropriate standards and labels can contain relevant product information for consumers, and UNEP is concerned with standards and labels and gives encouragement to business schemes that enhance sustainable production and consumption, an issue addressed in Chapter 5. Other agencies are very experienced in standard setting, and in this context UNEP has some coordination with ISO.

In relation to sustainable consumption, there are also examples of UNEP cooperation with the UN Global Compact, and at least in some projects non-governmental organizations, such as CI and the World Wide Fund for Nature (WWF), are involved as well.[31] Given the crucial role of business in the Compact, one is sometimes left with the impression that it is a kind of private organization, but it is not.

The UN Global Compact was conceived by former UN General Secretary Kofi Annan in 2000, much to the dismay of some civil society organizations, but to the comfort of business and, above all, large global corporations. These companies enroll and make commitments on a voluntary basis, and business participation is crucial, but firms must comply with the principles of the organization. This is an example of soft regulation in an area where there is no traditional top-down public regulation to control business.[32] Setting agendas and raising awareness are instead the formula.

On the agenda of the UN Global Compact we also find sustainable consumption as one of ten universal social responsibility principles, because "businesses should undertake initiatives to promote greater environmental responsibility." It is important, though, that the UN Global Compact cover many policy fields and be guided by a general goal in principle, one by which "access to global information means that consumers are increasingly aware of where their goods come from and the conditions under which they are made,"[33] and its activities spill into many areas relevant to consumer protection.

In addition to joining other initiatives and projects, the UN Global Compact itself is a coordinating body and serves as one of the hubs in the area of sustainable consumption and consumer protection. In a basic sense, the organization enjoys the support of the UN system, and this provides many opportunities for serving as a catalyst of change through cooperation with other agencies to promote the principles of corporate citizenship. Cooperation is formalized with organizations taking part in the Compact's Inter-Agency Team – OHCHR, ILO, UNEP, United Nations Office on Drugs and Crime (UNODC), United Nations Development Programme (UNDP), UNIDO, and United Nations Entity for Gender Equality and the Empowerment of Women (UN Women).

UNIDO has been quite active in different partnerships, but not all of these organizations are strong in consumer policy, and many organizations that otherwise give priority to consumer policy have not joined the Compact and the team. The organizational principles underpinning the UN Global Compact are different from those governing the other organizations in the team, and the Compact's principles emphasize network rather than hierarchy, and norm building rather than rule making.[34] Thus other opportunities for coordination can be exploited, but these principles and the voluntary contributions of business are at odds with the typical working style of the older, established organizations, where there is a preference for adopting binding rules, for instance in the form of international conventions. In fact, such preferences are also articulated by the consumer movement.

However, the team members can provide important inputs into coordination, and they help implement policies agreed to in this forum, some of which pertain to consumer protection, some to sustainable consumption, or both. Some of the organizations also combine consumer policy with social, human rights or development policies, suggesting that coordination goes in many directions.

Coordination – between food, health and consumer policies

The WHO and FAO belong to a rather small group of prolific intergovernmental organizations with a strong commitment to important areas of consumer policy. In Chapter 3 we discussed activities run independently by each of them, and they have their own strongholds and are unchallenged in some areas of consumer policy. In addition, they share authority when coordinating efforts in areas of common interests, and sometimes they bring competing perspectives forward. It is not always clear, for instance, which organization takes the lead in coordinating policy and is responsible for its administration. In the case of the Codex Alimentarius Commission, FAO was the driving force, while in the case of the International Food Safety Authorities Network (INFOSAN), WHO seems to have taken a lead role.[35] It can always be disputed who plays the major role, but there is a sound tradition of cooperation between the two agencies.

Advanced forms of coordination are reached in the field of nutrition, a significant area of consumer policy that is highly regulated at the global level, and in which there are strong historical traditions of coordination and institution building. An overarching institution is the United Nations Standing Committee on Nutrition (UNSCN), located within the UN, with participation from several intergovernmental agencies and engaged in many issues on nutrition.[36] To set standards for all foods and all processes in food production, and thus ensure food quality and food safety, an organization with the Latin name Codex Alimentarius Commission was established by FAO in 1961, joined by WHO the year after, and began its work in 1963. As such, the commission is one of the oldest international institutions mandated to define rules to protect consumers, and despite its somewhat esoteric name, its work is of paramount importance to consumers round the world.

According to the statutes of the Codex Alimentarius Commission, article 1, the general goal is "protecting the health of the consumers and ensuring fair practices in the food trade."[37] Although not highly visible to consumers, standards in nutrition, food quality and labelling can be conceived of as important public goods that are not just a guarantee for safe foods, when correctly implemented, but in a wider perspective are essential to building trust, and which therefore enable the globalization of food production and consumption. Concern for consumers plays a central role, but standards are also important for the food industry. With standard setting aiming to establish a level playing field, competition between firms in the food industry is regulated. Of course, there can be disagreement in the relevant industries, and also between the producer and consumer side, when defining nutrition and health standards.[38]

The status of the commission is complex. It can be considered an independent organization with its own members and rules, but its secretariat is run by FAO, and both FAO and WHO are the founding organizations and the key agencies behind the commission today. FAO and WHO deliver the primary strategies and sources of knowledge to develop policies, define procedures and establish standards, and the arrangement must mainly be understood in this context, but coordination includes a number of other intergovernmental agencies whose inputs are indispensable to the commission.

Science is not always king, as the controversy around genetically modified organisms (GMO) has shown. A now-dissolved task force under the commission was established to examine the implications of this technology for food safety, and it could only "treat the subject from a pure scientific perspective,"[39] somehow indicating that commercial interests are also at stake and can complicate policy formation. However, science provides a legitimate background for regulation and is crucially needed to establish sound criteria for food standards. Scientists from relevant areas are invited into the work of the commission, which is further supported by a variety of subsidiary bodies and some joint FAO/WHO bodies focusing on food additives, pesticide residues and risk analysis. In sum, a sizable administration, including a huge number of committees, working groups and task forces, is available to advance consumer protection, and its work is meticulously regulated in a procedural manual.

What is also regulated are the relations with external actors. Because significant attention is given to consumers, as well as to the food industry, it is logical to have formal relations with the affected interests. This strategy is codified in a set of "Principles Concerning the Participation of International Non-Governmental Organizations in the Work of the Codex Alimentarius Commission."[40] Similar principles exist in FAO and WHO. These principles offer consumer organizations opportunities to take part in much of the work, and consumers have participated in this forum as observers for many years. Rule-making is so complex and encompassing that it is difficult to build up the required expert knowledge and play an active role in all corners of food standards, but today there are consumer groups with special competencies in food safety. This will be discussed in Chapter 5. Consumer participation is clearly welcomed and encouraged, but still there are barriers that cannot be regulated away.

The Codex Alimentarius Commission covers major areas of nutrition policy, but there are issues that are not managed by the commission but are still subject to coordination between FAO and WHO. Especially since the late 1990s, the two organizations have jointly examined the problems of obesity as a lifestyle disease.[41] Tobacco smoking is also considered a lifestyle disease, and alone WHO has successfully developed strategies to inform consumers on the basis of the WHO Framework Convention on Tobacco Control, and eventually led many people to abandon smoking. Obesity, however, is related to nutritional problems, and defined by the FAO and WHO as a modern epidemic demanding action on behalf of governments and international agencies. Clearly there is an element of "standard setting" even here, as scientific agreement is required to define obesity as a disease, in this case a non-communicable disease. Global strategies are devised by FAO and WHO to combat obesity, governments are offered various analyses and tools to implement them, and growing pressure is put on food and beverage companies to develop new and alternative products and provide better information for consumers to make a healthy choice.[42] With a growing part of the world population becoming obese, not just in the developed countries, these strategies appeal to growing masses of consumers. Efforts are currently being made by the World Obesity Federation and CI to have FAO and WHO adopt a convention "to protect and promote healthy diets,"[43]and thus follow up the High-level Meeting of the UN General Assembly on the Prevention and Control of Non-communicable Diseases, held in 2011.

Conclusion

Advancing consumer protection is not always a matter of winning contributions from single organizations, whether we analyze bodies that formulate strategies to the betterment of consumers in all markets, or focus on agencies that concentrate on particular sectors of the economy. Many challenges cannot be addressed on this basis alone, and consequently a number of organizations are involved in coordination with other agencies – sometimes spanning several entities in *ad hoc* networks, sometimes just involving a few central bodies. In this chapter we have concentrated on major cases of inter-agency coordination that are comparatively advanced and represent different fields of consumer policy, and we have met some of the "usual suspects" from the previous chapters which, to various degrees, bring their own traditions and approaches into coordination. Their capacities are essential in fostering coordination.

First, various policy clusters around both general and specific areas of consumer policy can be identified in coordination. Global consumer policies have evolved around certain issues, industries and consumer demands, where good opportunities and bold actions have been combined, but other areas have been left behind or remained completely untouched. Areas where coordination of consumer protection has made progress are general principles governing consumer protection, food and health, trade and development, sustainability and education. Some of these areas are really pioneers, such as food and health, where coordination goes back to the early 1960s with separate institutions and strong paradigms; others are far less developed, such as sustainable consumption, where coordination developed quite recently. Certainly, the development of many of the policy clusters listed here still leaves much to be desired, and implementation is weak, with huge disparities around the world.

Second, coordination brings together a variety of agencies in different policy clusters, and while all these bodies include consumer protection as one of their goals, the role of consumer policy in the clusters varies. In some cases, consumer protection is the overriding concern and there is a clear mandate to give priority to this, whereas in other cases consumer protection is one of several goals, as for instance in trade, and there is a struggle between different principles. Alone, the language of competition policy is not sufficient to forward the consumer cause, and this is a barrier in some of the clusters. However, this is not always detrimental to consumer policy. Indeed, the combination with issues such as sustainability, development and education offers new opportunities that would hardly be available if consumer agendas were isolated and travelled alone.

Third, coordination is associated with the integration of complementary resources from the participating organizations, and even with a willingness to learn from each other, but coordination is also related to various "turf wars," in which there are struggles between institutions and interests. However, the organizations are not always taking an active part in coordination, as the revising of the UN guidelines illustrates, although they have here an opportunity to defend their approaches and turfs. As a matter of fact the organizations have many commitments other than consumer policy and do not always give it sufficient attention. In established areas of coordination, such as food and health or trade, the organizations may have different approaches, but they are at least familiar with potential conflicts and boundaries, while in new areas, such as financial education, the domains of the organizations are still not established.

Coordination can take many forms, and a variety of roles are attributed to the participating agencies. This suggests that coordination is an encompassing category that must be broken down into specific subtypes, and this chapter offers insights into only some of them. Theories are not sufficiently developed to account for the diversity in inter-agency coordination. From a theoretical perspective it is, however, important to examine the different incentives for coordination, as organizations may have reasons to both seek and avoid coordination. Many different intergovernmental organizations meet each other in coordination, but in several cases coordination includes an additional group of external parties, and we have occasionally referred to this when relevant. Chapter 5 devotes full attention to the consumer side and the business side, showing how these are organized and what kinds of contribution they make to the development of consumer policy at the global level.

Notes

1 United Nations General Assembly, *Set of Multilaterally Agreed Equitable Principles and Rules for the Control of Restrictive Business Practices*, Resolution 35/63 (December 1980).
2 Robin Brown, *The UN Guidelines for Consumer Protection. Making them Work in Developing Countries*, paper for Consumers' International Congress 2011 (Yarralumla: Foundation for Effective Markets and Governance, 2011).
3 UNCTAD, *Ad Hoc Expert Meeting on Consumer Protection: The Interface between Competition and Consumer Policies*, http://unctad.org/en/Pages/MeetingDetails.aspx?meetingid=65.
4 UNCTAD, *Implementation Report. United Nations Guidelines for Consumer Protection (1985–2013)*, Intergovernmental Group of Experts on Competition Law and Policy, Thirteenth session, United Nations TD/B/C. I/CLP/ (Geneva: UNCTAD, July 2013).
5 UNCTAD, *United Nations Guidelines on Consumer Protection*, http://unctad.org/en/Pages/DITC/CompetitionLaw/UN-Guidelines-on-Consumer-Protection.aspx.
6 UNCTAD (Trade and Development Board), *Expert Meeting on Consumer Interests, Competitiveness, Competition and Development*, Geneva, 17–19 October 2001. List of participants TD/B/COM.1/EM.17/INF.1, 24 October 2001.
7 It has a stronger role in other areas: Martha Finnemore, "International organizations as teachers of norms: the United Nations Educational, Scientific and Cultural Organization and Science Policy," *International Organization* 47, no. 4 (1993): 565–97.
8 OECD, *Improving Financial Literacy: Analysis of Issues and Policies* (Paris: Organisation for Economic Co-operation and Development, 2005); OECD, *Promoting Consumer Education Trends, Policies and Good Practices: Trends, Policies and Good Practices* (Paris: Organisation for Economic Co-operation and Development, 2009).
9 Another example of inter-agency coordination around consumer education is found in tourism (United Nations Decade on Education for Sustainable Development 2005–2014). Coordination is through an inter-agency committee attended by other agencies including UNEP, ILO, UNICEF, United Nations University (UNU), Joint United Nations Programme on HIV/

AIDS (UNAIDS), World Food Programme (WFP), United Nations Human Settlements Programme (UN Habitat) as well as the World Bank.

10 This area has only recently been examined. Lisa Kastner, "'Much ado about nothing?' Transnational civil society, consumer protection and financial regulatory reform," *Review of International Political Economy* 21, no. 6 (2014): 1313–45; Peter Cartwright, "Understanding and protecting vulnerable financial consumers," *Journal of Consumer Policy*, online 13 December 2014.

11 World Bank, *Good Practices for Financial Consumer Protection* (Washington, DC: World Bank, 2012).

12 The "Joint Forum" provides coordination between the Basel Committee on Banking Supervision (BCBS), the International Organization of Securities Commissions (IOSCO) and the International Association of Insurance Supervisors (IAIS). It brings together experiences and formulates principles and practices that have a bearing on consumers. The Joint Forum was established in 1996.

13 OECD, *International Gateway for Financial Education, About*, www.financial-education.org/about.html.

14 OECD and G20, *Advancing National Strategies for Financial Education* (Paris: Organisation for Economic Co-operation and Development, 2013), 37.

15 G20, *G20 Financial Inclusion Action Plan*, Financial Inclusion Experts Group. Adopted at the G20 Seoul Summit, December 2010.

16 OECD, *G20 High-Level Principles on Financial Consumer Protection* (Paris: Organisation for Economic Co-operation and Development, 2011).

17 CI, *Safe, Fair and Competitive Markets in Financial Services: Recommendations for the G20 on the Enhancement of Consumer Protection in Financial Services*, www.consumersinternational.org/media/669348/cifinancialreport2011.pdf.

18 OECD and G20, *Advancing National Strategies for Financial Education* (Paris: Organisation for Economic Co-operation and Development, 2013). The Russian G20 Presidency played an important part in the preparation of this report.

19 Tim Büthe, "The politics of food safety in the age of global trade: the Codex Alimentarius Commission in the SPS-Agreement of the WTO," in *Import Safety: Regulatory Governance in the Global Economy*, ed. Cary Coglianese, Adam Finkel and David Zaring (Philadelphia: University of Pennsylvania Press, 2009), 88–109.

20 The same status is attributed to the World Organization for Animal Health (OIE) and the International Plant Protection Convention (IPPC).

21 Steve Charnovitz, "The supervision of health and biosafety regulation by world trade rules," *Tulane Environmental Law Journal* 13, (2000): 271–302.

22 For a critique from the consumer movement see Lori Wallach and Michelle Sforza, *Whose Trade Organization: Corporate Globalization and the Erosion of Democracy* (Washington, DC: Public Citizen, 1999).

23 CI, *Decision Making in the Global Market: Trade, Standards and the Consumer* (London: Consumers International, 2005).

24 Christian J. Tams and Christian Tietje, eds, *Documents in International Economic Law: Trade, Investment and Finance* (Oxford: Oxford University Press, 2012).

25 Marie-Laure Djelic and Thibaut Kleiner, "The international competition network – moving towards transnational governance," in *Transnational*

Governance: Institutional Dynamics of Regulation, eds Marie-Laure Djelic and Kerstin Sahlin-Andersson (Cambridge: Cambridge University Press, 2006), 287–307. Here "transnational" alludes to the activities beyond nation states, but not to those of private actors.

26 International Competition Network, *Factsheet and Key Messages*, April 2009.

27 This includes the following departments and organizations, some of which have a comparatively strong profile in consumer protection: DESA (UN), UNIDO, UNCTAD, UNDP, FAO, ILO, UN-Habitat, WHO, UNESCO and UNWTO, www.unep.org/10yfp/ActorsStructure/Secretariat/tabid/106251/ Default.aspx.

28 UNEP, *Here and Now! Education for Sustainable Consumption: Recommendations and Guidelines* (Nairobi: UNEP, 2010). In this process the Consumer Citizen Network (CCN), in which UNEP and UNESCO – and Consumers International – participate, made important contributions. Victoria W. Thoresen, ed., *Consumer Citizenship Education: Guidelines* (Elverum: Consumer Citizenship Network, 2005).

29 The inter-agency committee has 22 UN organizations as members: Global Compact, Convention on Biological Diversity (CBD), DESA, ILO, FAO, UNESCO, WHO, World Bank, UN Convention to Combat Desertification (UNCCD), WTO, UNDP, UNEP, Office of the United Nations High Commissioner for Refugees (UNHCR), UNICEF, United Nations Population Fund (UNFPA), WFP, UN-Habitat, United Nations Office for Disaster Reduction (UNISDR), UNAIDS, UNFCCC, United Nations Institute for Training and Research (UNITAR) and UNU, www.unesco.org/new/en/unesco/events/all-events/?tx_browser_pi1%5BshowUid%5D=26916&cHash=3270ffa18b.

30 UNEP, *Communication and Marketing,* www.unep.org/resourceefficiency/Home/Society/CommunicationandMarketing/tabid/101265/Default.aspx.

31 UNEP, UN Global Compact and Utopies, *Talk the Walk: Advancing Sustainable Lifestyles through Marketing and Communications* (Nairobi: UNEP, 2005).

32 The Compact is widely researched. Although it has the potential to advance business responsibility, this privatization of governance has also been critically evaluated. Susanne Soederberg, "Taming corporations or buttressing market-led development? A critical assessment of the Global Compact," *Globalizations* 4, no. 4 (2007): 500–13; Jackie Smith, "Power, interests, and the United Nations Global Compact," in *The Challenges of Global Business Authority. Democratic Renewal, Stalemate, or Decay?*, eds Tony Porter and Karsten Ronit (Albany: State University of New York Press, 2010), 89–113.

33 UN Global Compact, *The Ten Principles*, www.unglobalcompact.org/AboutTheGC/TheTenPrinciples/index.html. Some of these ideas are expressed in the United Nations Guiding Principles on Business and Human Rights (UNGPs) adopted in 2011 by the United Nations Human Rights Council. John G. Ruggie, *Just Business. Multinational Corporations and Human Rights* (New York: W.W. Norton, 2013).

34 Steve Waddell, *The Global Compact: An Organizational Innovation to Realize UN Principles*, paper presented at the Global Compact Donor Group Meeting, 26 October 2011.

35 WHO, *WHO Global Strategy for Food Safety: Safer Food for Better Health* (Geneva: WHO, 2002). INFOSAN was established a few years later in 2004.

36 Also UNICEF is engaged in nutrition issues, especially with regard to children.

37 *Statutes of the Codex Alimentarius Commission* (Adopted in 1961 by the 11th Session of the FAO Conference and in 1963 by the 16th Session of the World Health Assembly. Revised in 1966 and 2006).

38 Industry leverage is analyzed in relation to particularly aggressive campaigns, an example being the international activities of the sugar industry. Sarah Boseley, "Political context of the World Health Organization: sugar industry threatens to scupper the WHO," *International Journal of Health Services* 33, no. 4 (2003): 831–3.

39 FAO, *Introduction to Biosecurity*, www.fao.org/biosecurity.

40 WHO/FAO, *Procedural Manual Codex Alimentarius Commission*, 22nd edn (Rome: WHO/FAO, 2014).

41 WHO, *Obesity: Preventing and Managing the Global Epidemic* (Geneva: World Health Organization, 2000).

42 Youfa Wang and Tim Lobstein, "Worldwide trends in childhood overweight and obesity," *International Journal of Pediatric Obesity* 1, no. 1. (2006): 11–25; Karsten Ronit and Jørgen Dejgård Jensen, "Obesity and industry self-regulation of food and beverage marketing: a literature review," *European Journal of Clinical Nutrition* 68, no. 4 (2014): 753–59.

43 World Obesity Federation, *Over 320 International Experts and Civil Society Groups Call for a Binding Treaty to Tackle Poor Diets*, press release, 17 November 2014.

5 Private organizations: consumers and business

- General consumer organizations in the consumer movement
- Special organizations in and around the consumer movement
- General business associations engaged in consumer policy
- Special business associations and related bodies engaged in consumer policy
- Conclusion

It is a major argument of this chapter, and of this book, that the role of different private organizations must be integrated into any study on global consumer organizations. In the previous chapters brief reference was made to the participation of these actors in the work of many agencies and the formal regulation of this participation, but more attention is required to describe and analyze the different roles performed by private organizations and the activities that unfold beyond the purview of intergovernmental organizations.

This analysis adds further complexity to the study, and if the community of intergovernmental organizations appears relatively fragmented, this fragmentation is nothing compared with that in the world of private organizations engaged in global consumer policy. There are many private organizations and activities, and these are dynamic and mutating and not easy to capture; for this reason we concentrate on the engagement of major organizations. There are, however, a further group of actors that are usually of an ephemeral character and that are involved mainly in campaigning activities. And on top of that, we find organizations who are concerned with other issues, such as human rights or climate change, and do not define their strategies in terms of consumer protection, but who nevertheless have some impact on the conditions of consumers.

Yet there is a huge variation between consumer organizations representing consumers and those representing business. The former group works on behalf of consumers, whereas the latter group, whilst it addresses consumer issues, represents various firms and industries. On the consumer side, fragmentation is strong and many smaller outfits exist, but interest representation is also characterized by a high degree of centralization. The chapter, therefore, focuses on different groups in the consumer movement. Notwithstanding certain failures to organize the many and diverse consumer interests, it is amazing that a number of formal organizations have been created to represent consumers at the global level. Theories do not adequately explain the complex mechanisms underlying such large entities, but we seek to offer some explanations for the emergence and maintenance of some formal organizations of consumers.

On the business side, there are many organizations that represent different industries and product groups, but some organizations have a coordinating role. In some cases business associations and other entities formulate norms and rules for business self-regulation, and civil society organizations may take part in business self-regulation by designing and managing arrangements. There has been much skepticism as to whether there is really the potential in business to create and administer rules in consumer protection, and as to whether business self-regulation can be seen as a legitimate tool in consumer protection. Theories point to several shortcomings in such arrangements, but also note many accomplishments by organized business, sometimes in cooperation with civil society.

The various private organizations have different strategies and play many roles in relation to consumer protection: they set and influence agendas and leverage intergovernmental organizations, as well as the regulation adopted through these agencies. Some of these aspects are discussed in previous chapters. But under specific circumstances, private organizations are capable of providing alternative forms of governance, often in areas where public regulation is weak and underdeveloped.

The two sides of the market – consumers and business – have very different organizational systems. In this chapter we first look at the general consumer organizations in the form of Consumers International (CI), then examine some specific consumer organizations that in principle strive for the very same interests, but only in relation to specific markets and industries. The second part of the chapter deals with those business associations that have shown an active interest in the formulation of principles for business and have adopted rules that explicitly address the situation of consumers. Again, we first study the general associations, including the International Chamber of Commerce (ICC), then move on to specific industry associations that attend to consumer issues in some specific areas and to other entities that, together with business, are engaged in areas of self-regulation that have a bearing on consumers. Finally, we consider the consequences of these patterns for the structures of global consumer policy.

General consumer organizations in the consumer movement

The organization and representation of consumers at the global level may seem a conundrum. Is it really possible to organize such diverse interests and so many people? A basic problem is how to bring together an extremely large group under some meaningful common denominator, identify key challenges, and sustain cooperation over time through formal organizations.[1] Exacerbating these structural challenges, the uneven economic development in the world brings much heterogeneity into the consumer community. The socio-economic background of consumers is very different: some live in wealthy societies with an abundance of consumer goods and with complex patterns of consumption, whereas others strive to keep up a basic subsistence, with very little purchasing power and a focus on basic foods. This is the situation facing global consumer organizations in general; they can mitigate problems and overcome such challenges when they respect diversity and balance different consumer concerns. In terms of collective action theory, it is important that the organizations representing consumers be considered legitimate by key interlocutors, thus the sheer number of members is not decisive,[2] but this recognition must be obtained in a global context.

The leading international consumer organization is CI.[3] CI is structured as a large federation consisting of mainly national consumer organizations, and therefore is not based on direct membership of individual consumers. Founded in 1960, it was a child of the affluent society – and also of the consumer society – in which different civil society groups gained a voice and began to influence politics in areas hitherto dominated by business. It became a goal for many governments to listen to this no longer "silent majority," and this development spilled over to the international level, as described in Chapter 1.

The ambition of CI is to represent all consumers on all continents, and "to support, develop and work directly with our constituent member organizations."[4] A significant number of national associations and other entities are today affiliated with the CI – more than 240 in 120 countries.[5] With regard to funding, an interesting aspect is that the CI has a quite remarkable stock of affiliate members comprising various government agencies. They pay fees, but have no voting rights.

Over many years CI has been able to solidify its own position as a world-encompassing organization by actively assisting in the building of new associations in countries where national associations are non-existent and civil society is not particularly well organized, and where governments have done very little to encourage the organization of consumers.[6] This is the case in many countries in Africa, Asia and Latin America. With reference to the articles on participation in the International Bill of Human Rights (Universal Declaration of Human Rights, International Covenant on Civil and Political Rights and International Covenant on Economic, Social and Cultural Rights), as well as specific consumer-related documents, CI strives to improve the situation.

The global organization of consumers is therefore characterized by a dual movement of bottom-up and top-down processes. Explained in a somewhat simplified way, consumer organizations from the affluent parts of the world originally founded CI, and later CI helped with the establishment of consumer organizations in the developing countries. This is a critical factor for CI, because it needs global coverage to assert itself as a global actor in consumer policy and to become recognized by intergovernmental organizations and business alike. It teaches us some important lessons about the conditions for organizing civil society at the global level more generally, and it tells a fascinating story about the challenges facing consumers more specifically, and how to compensate for the barriers to collective action. The federated structure, although not solving all recruitment problems, has proved to be a useful formula for the coordination of interests on a global scale, and such coherence is generally an important aspect of leverage in global politics.

Although CI has a broad constituency, it is in many ways a secretariat-driven organization. Few national member associations have experience with the work of intergovernmental organizations and global issues, but its secretariat, based in London (UK) and supported by regional offices in Santiago de Chile, Pretoria, Kuala Lumpur and Azaiba (Oman), disposes of professional experts in many areas of consumer protection. Occasionally, the organization also draws on input from external consultants.

The organization is focused on building up this expertise to participate in many institutional contexts rather than relying on the charisma of high-profile individuals. Not that the CI has been without strong personalities in its leadership, but its style is very different from that of consumer organizations driven by individual policy entrepreneurs – recall Ralph Nader's historical role in the American consumer movement, or the more recent example of the no-logo program initiated by Canadian Naomi Klein.[7]

Strategic emphasis is on advocating a number of consumer rights and responsibilities, as listed in Box 5.1.

Box 5.1 Consumer rights and responsibilities in the perspective of CI

Rights:

- The right to the satisfaction of basic needs
- The right to safety
- The right to be informed
- The right to choose
- The right to be heard
- The right to redress
- The right to consumer education
- The right to a healthy environment

Responsibilities:

- Critical awareness
- Involvement or action
- Social responsibility
- Ecological responsibility
- Solidarity

CI, Consumer Rights: www.consumersinternational.org
/who-we-are/consumer-rights.

The provision of knowledge-based input into the making of global consumer policy is organized around different intergovernmental agencies.[8] Consumers International has to match the expertise hosted both in these agencies and in business, although this is not always achievable because CI disposes of far fewer resources, but it is an organization that keeps track of many developments. Given this broad commitment, it spans a wider field than any other international organization, including the different intergovernmental bodies, each of which concentrates on a more narrow field of issues. That also applies to organizations such as UNCTAD and the OECD, and illustrates the comparative strength of CI.

CI has developed expertise in a rich diversity of policy fields. Of primary importance is the ability to address the basic principles of consumer protection, particularly with regard to the UN Guidelines for Consumer Protection, a centerpiece in global consumer policy, and other documents outlining the rights of consumers. The adoption and revision of such principles are important both in their own right, and in a wider perspective because they can serve as a guidance for consumer protection in specific areas. CI has displayed significant stamina in the deliberations on consumer policy and in hammering out general rules, as we saw in Chapter 4.

CI was instrumental in raising this discussion in the 1960s, 1970s and 1980s, and in formulating principles that later became official policy in the UN and other international bodies. Also, the current revision of the UN Guidelines for Consumer Protection is very closely followed by CI, as is a range of broad consumer issues including development, education and sustainability, some of which are actually part of the guidelines and have the profound interest of CI.

In addition to formulating general strategies, CI is involved in special areas of consumer policy, therefore it cannot be seen as a general organization dedicated mainly to the broad ideals and general protection of consumers, leaving various sectoral matters to specialized organizations and other groups. It is the combination of tasks and the broad experience derived from many consumer issues and regulations that enables CI to synthesize these into wide-ranging global strategies to protect consumers. CI has been involved in many issue areas for decades. Today its policy portfolio covers major sectors including food, telecommunications and financial services,[9] but many more issues could be added and CI seems to move in and out of the different fields according to the attention they need at any given time. This capacity is an inherent feature of CI strategy and gives it a unique position in the consumer movement.

It has always been a chief goal of CI to become recognized and gain observer status in intergovernmental organizations, or at least in bodies of relevance to consumers. This recognition brings many advantages, from access to various categories of documents, to different consultation rights, to the inclusion in relevant bodies where consumer policy is deliberated. Not all agencies are open to participation by non-governmental organizations, however, and here CI faces the same problem as any other organization. However, many agencies have welcomed consumer participation, and over recent decades several bodies have revised their strategies to become more transparent and inclusive, and new activities have emerged beyond the official meetings. The emphasis on participation is related to CI's ambition to enhance consumer protection through public regulation. CI has a strong preference for principles and strategies adopted at the intergovernmental level and implemented by governments, and does not believe in the many voluntary commitments of business: there is a risk that firms will free-ride, and it is difficult to monitor and sanction non-compliance.

Many intergovernmental organizations employ the same principles of recognition, with some adaptations to suit specific institutional demands,[10] and essentially only associations with a wide membership base, and at best near-global, are eligible and will be granted consultative status. There is a formal admission process in which the properties of the applicant organizations will be scrutinized. It is of overriding importance that usually only one organization per interest category be admitted, and agencies will proceed critically to avoid recognizing competing organizations with similar constituencies, as they may bring conflicting input into the organizations and in one way or another complicate decision-making.

Therefore the principles and preferences of the agencies have an impact on private organizations engaged in consumer policy, and CI has achieved a special status as the most representative outlet for consumers. There is no competing organization with the same representative character, let alone the same knowledge base and expertise, so this choice has never been difficult. However, the basic principle to recognize organizations with primarily a global activity has of course been an additional driver for the CI in organizing consumers in those parts of the world with weak civil society institutions and a strong need for capacity building. Interestingly, several agencies assist in this process, and it is one of the official goals of organizations such as UNCTAD and the World Bank to develop appropriate regulatory authorities and domestic consumer organizations, a development that is helpful to CI-organizing interests. This forms part of a complex model of collective action where several institutional conditions must be factored in.[11]

In previous chapters we referred to the formal participation of the consumer movement, and of CI in particular. Table 5.1 shows where CI has achieved consultative status or other forms of accreditation.[12]

There is no organization with a mission and profile similar to the CI's, but there are a few other general organizations that have a narrower program and constituency. The International Co-operative Alliance (ICA) and one of its many sections, Consumer Cooperatives Worldwide (CCW), is based on the distinct idea of the cooperative movement. It has a unique agenda that is different from the CI mission, which is critical of all kinds of market dysfunctions but does not advocate any particular kind of ownership model to advance consumer

Table 5.1 Current status of Consumers International in international agencies

Organization	Status
United Nations – ECOSOC	General consultative status
United Nations Conference on Trade and Development (UNCTAD)	General consultative status
Organization for Economic Cooperation and Development (OECD)	Special consultative status
International Organization for Standardization (ISO) (International Electrotechnical Commission, IEC)	Liaison organization to ISO
World Intellectual Property Organization (WIPO)	Observer status
Food and Agriculture Organization (FAO)	Specialized consultative status
World Health Organization (WHO)	Official relations
Codex Alimentarius Commission (and various committees)	Observer status
United Nations Educational, Scientific and Cultural Organization (UNESCO)	General consultative status
United Nations Industrial Development Organization (UNIDO)	General consultative status
International Telecommunication Union (ITU)	ITU Telecommunication Development Sector – CI is a member
United Nations Environment Program (UNEP)	General consultative status

CI, Accreditation, www.consumersinternational.org/our-members/join-us!/accreditation/

interests. Various other international organizations with a regional membership base launch their own activities and stand out as independent entities but have close cooperation with CI. This applies, for instance, to the Transatlantic Consumer Dialogue (TACD), created in 1998 to deliver input into US–EU trade negotiations and the institutional framework established to that end.[13] This task is coordinated by CI. Another example is the Consumer Unity & Trust Society (CUTS), established in India in 1983, with offices in other countries, which is driven by the explicit goal of representing consumers in the poor countries.[14] It is engaged in a number of issues pertaining to consumers, and has been successful in achieving consultancy status or otherwise building relations with relevant intergovernmental organizations, primarily with UNCTAD. It is worth noting that CUTS is a member of CI. That these other platforms exist does not appear to weaken CI, but rather gives it additional strength.

CI entertains relations with a variety of civil society organizations that are not consumer organizations *per se*,[15] but that cater to certain consumer demands and define strategies with regard to specific products and services. A number of environmental and human rights organizations, for instance, address certain fringes of consumer protection without seeing themselves as consumer organizations, and at the same time we are seeing CI and other consumer groups move into new areas and add new aspects to consumer policy. These developments make coordination between the consumer movement and other civil society organizations relevant and pave the way for alliance building. These intersections bring interesting dynamics into the organization of consumers, and redefine consumer policy.

Special organizations in and around the consumer movement

The CI is a major catalyst for collective consumer action at the global level, and also assists in various regional and national contexts. However, there are various smaller and independent organizations that concentrate on specific areas and are recognized within their respective domains without taking up broader issues in consumer protection.[16] They do not always see themselves as belonging to a movement, but their special work is often a supplement to that of the key organization; overlaps do exist, and to different degrees coordination is sought. Many smaller initiatives with some consumer perspective on the agenda, however, are living their own life and are typically organized around particular segments of consumers, markets and products; they are not necessarily operating at the global level, although they have an ambition to influence global developments. They are facing problems of collective action, and more research is necessary to understand these groups in the consumer movement.

There is a huge variation between special organizations in the consumer movement. Table 5.2 lists examples of specialized global consumer organizations which are related to three areas of global consumer policy discussed in Chapter 3, namely food, health and air transport.

Each of the consumer-good categories listed in Table 5.2 is complex and comprises many items, but there are designated consumer organizations to advance the interests of consumers in each area. The commodities in the selected categories are not equally relevant to, and purchased by, all consumers around the world, but the examples

Table 5.2 Special organizations in the consumer movement

Goods and services	Organization	Founded	Policy fields	Relations with intergovern-mental organizations
Food	International Association of Consumer Food Organi-zations (IACFO)	1997	Consumer policy Food policy Trade policy	WHO, WTO, FAO, Codex Alimentarius Commission, OECD
Health	Health Action International (HAI)	1981	Consumer policy	WHO
	International Alliance of Patients' Organizations (IAPO)	1999	Health policy	ECOSOC
Air transport	International Airline Passen-gers Associa-tion (IAPA)	1960 (as the Air-ways Club)	Different issues but mainly a service organization	Weak relations with agencies

Sources: http://cspinet.org/International/iacfo.html; www.haiweb.org; https://iapo.org.uk; www.iapa.com.

display some important features of globalization and show that initiatives have emerged to influence regulation and to challenge business.

One of the special organizations engaged in consumer policy is the International Association of Consumer Food Organizations (IACFO), whose secretariat is run by the Washington-based Center for Science in the Public Interest (CSPI), and which is further engaged in another initiative, Safe Food International.[17] The members of IACFO are a mixed bag, including a number of national consumer groups from developing countries and the International Baby Food Action Network (IBFAN). In a way, it is an encompassing association in the sense that it addresses a broad range of food products, a huge area where much technical expertise is required to formulate strategies and to monitor compliance with standards at different stages of the production chain. It covers a number of industries and concentrates on classical issues in consumer protection such as safety, standards and trade. Food is an area where much competence is found in the public sector and in intergovernmental organizations, but it is the task of IACFO to bring the consumer perspective more strongly into public debate and into regulation.

However, food is a basic commodity and very regulated compared with other products, and is also one of the traditional focal areas of CI. Therefore it is quite complicated for IACFO as a new association to move into a traditional field in consumer policy and become a recognized player, but the organization has succeeded in establishing a number of relations with different agencies, first and foremost the Codex Alimentarius. The appearance of IACFO does not in any way imply that CI has now scaled down its activities in the field, or surrendered it to IACFO, but the involvement of different organizations can give rise to conflicts about the representation of interests.

The global health policy community is also highly institutionalized, with a rich diversity of public and private organizations. We even find organizations that to some extent have the character of consumer organizations, but, as in other cases, it is difficult to establish and maintain associations to represent consumers. A key organization with a comparatively strong membership and knowledge base is Health Action International (HAI). It has its headquarters in Amsterdam but also has offices in Africa, Asia-Pacific and Europe, so it qualifies as a global actor. In certain respects it sees itself as a Dutch organization, although it has multiple identities, and its global activities span different issues related to medicine, such as consumer education, pricing, promotion and safety matters, all classical topics in the regulation of drugs. Health Action International is occupied with many of the same issues that the WHO is struggling with, and it combines perspectives on health and consumer policy in its many relations with the WHO, which is actually one of its donors.

A more recently established organization is the International Alliance of Patients Organizations (IAPO), which builds on a number of existing national associations. Within only a few years it has become engaged in a broad array of health care issues, some pertaining to the role of patients in public health care systems, others addressing patients as consumers in their relations with the private sector. Its primary objective is to seek influence on the situation of consumers worldwide and on the way this is regulated in the context of intergovernmental agencies, especially the WHO. Individual services to consumers, however, fall largely beyond the remit of IAPO.

The International Airline Passengers Association (IAPA) is a very different kind of association, displaying the diversity of organizations in the broad consumer movement. From its offices in London, Dallas,

Hong Kong and Dubai,[18] it offers different kinds of service to individual travellers, but is also concerned with how to "protect" the interests of airline travellers, primarily the "frequent business travellers" whose interests it caters to rather than the huge group of airline passengers around the world. Therefore we can neither characterize IAPA as a representative organization for this broad segment of consumers, nor describe it as an organization with explicit political goals to enhance consumer protection in the specialized policy community of air travel. The organization comments on a number of consumer issues through position papers, with a bias toward the situation in the USA, but interestingly it does not refer to the work of ICAO as the relevant UN agency in air transport, or to IATA as the organization of airline companies. Few contacts are recorded with the ICAO as the key regulatory body in international aviation, and IAPA does not attend the ICAO assembly as an observer.[19]

In addition to these three examples, characterized by different organizational designs, there are a number of other initiatives with a global orientation that do not refer primarily to consumer protection, or that do not always seek to organize consumers, but nevertheless include a consumer perspective on regulation. These initiatives concentrate on certain products and industries using different strategies of participation and protest, and, in some cases, establish themselves as knowledge organizations.

It has been extremely difficult to find a suitable format for regulating the internet and involving different stakeholders. In this institutional development, however, some actors have emerged as representing consumers, and today the Non-Commercial Users Constituency (NCUC) is the platform for ordinary users of the internet, and is one of the formal constituencies in the machinery of the Internet Corporation for Assigned Names and Numbers (ICANN); ICANN Watch also plays a role. The NCUC does not draw significantly on the general language of consumer policy, however. The same applies to another organization, Intellectual Property Watch, founded in 2004, which is monitoring international developments in the broad field of intellectual property policy, with an emphasis on industries of critical importance.

Some actors also advocate for different kinds of "justice." The Tax Justice Network (TJN), established in 2003, is involved in analysing and criticizing tax policy and financial regulation, especially the tax evasion of multinational corporations, with which it has had much success; it combines knowledge building and activism, and leverages relevant international agencies. These activities have some relevance for consumers, but TJN is not an initiative that in any way comes near to being a consumer group in the financial sector. At a more general level, Transparency International advocates for greater openness in the public and private sectors, and these activities also challenge business and have potential benefits for consumers, although the organization is not geared toward consumer issues as such.

Finally, we should mention that initiatives by general environmental and human rights organizations, such as the efforts of Human Rights Watch to stop child labor in various industries and countries, or the work of WWF to enhance sustainable consumption, can make important contributions in some areas of consumer policy without qualifying as consumer organizations proper. Again, this work may be appreciated by certain consumer segments. It urges corporations to behave more responsibly and provide better information, and eventually to enable all consumers to make a more informed choice. Some of these bold initiatives are managed jointly by civil society groups outside the traditional consumer movement and business, or by business alone, as discussed below.

General business associations engaged in consumer policy

The global business community is characterized by a much more diversified organizational landscape than is the consumer side. Business is strongly organized at the global level, which enables both large and encompassing organizations, as well as a plethora of specific industry associations, to engage in various areas of consumer policy.[20] Obviously, business associations do not organize or represent consumers. However, they are active in global consumer policy, with activities driven by incentives to create the necessary regulatory infrastructures for business operations, to enhance the competitiveness and reputation of business, and to respond to pressures from consumers and regulators. These different entities are not only capable of formulating strategies and leveraging political institutions. The discretionary power of business to manufacture and market products and services, within certain limits set by public regulation, includes that businesses also have the opportunity to establish and join various forms of self-regulation. In such cases, norms and rules adopted by business, sometimes in cooperation with other interested parties, govern the behavior of firms in their relations with consumers.

We first turn to the peak associations active at the trans-industry level in global business, of which there are few. These organizations face the challenge of large-scale collective action, but the number of firms to be organized and represented is considerably smaller than the number of individual consumers, and global associations benefit from organizing national organizations rather than individual firms.

These peak associations have very different commitments to consumer policy, which is just one of many issue areas to be managed. The most significant of the global associations engaged in consumer affairs is indisputably the International Chamber of Commerce (ICC).[21] With national members in many countries around the globe, the ICC represents business in both the affluent and the developing countries, and it is very conscious about assisting business in building institutional capacities in countries where solid associations are missing. This broad coverage means that the ICC receives input from many countries and is updated about the situation for business, and well positioned to formulate global strategies. Its authority has many sources, and its high profile is attributable not only to the fact that it has members from many countries, but also to the circumstance that it harnesses significant resources and runs the largest secretariat of all the major global business associations.[22] The ICC therefore has a huge capacity to formulate new and independent initiatives, and at the same time to respond to a diversity of challenges from international agencies and a number of civil society organizations, including the consumer movement.

Today the ICC must be considered the world's largest business association and, as described in Chapter 1, its history and status go back a long way. Almost 100 years old, it has established itself as the leading organization in its field, and along the way it has not seriously encountered other associations with similar ambitions in the global business community. Furthermore, it has become recognized among intergovernmental organizations, and for many decades participated in the work of international agencies. The ICC has been granted consultative status and other forms of official recognition, which enables it to follow the work of these bodies very closely, giving the ICC a unique opportunity to further, or if necessary to block, initiatives that have a negative impact on business. It is typical, however, that participation is first and foremost sought and granted in relation to bodies with a broad focus on economic issues, and not to agencies that specialize in the regulation of specific industries. Such tasks are left mainly to associations representing specific sectors of business, but there are also several of these general intergovernmental bodies that, in one way or another, address consumer policy and therefore demand the perennial attention of the ICC.

Because of its considerable policy portfolio, the ICC is connected with consumer protection in many indirect ways, for instance in such issues as competition, trade, intellectual property rights, the digital economy and anti-corruption. Even in broader areas, such as investment and economic policy, the ICC can have an impact on policies deliberated and agreed in various global forums.

It is important to stress that the ICC is further involved in consumer policy in very explicit ways. Although it sees effective competition as a clear benefit to consumers, its efforts are not reducible to this argument, and the focus on competition is not a substitute for addressing consumer protection. The organization refers to consumers and finds it necessary to establish rules to safeguard the interests of consumers, but from the standpoint of business, which needs rules to regulate competition between firms in their relations with consumers. Some issues in consumer protection attract particular attention from the ICC. Marketing and advertising is clearly a stronghold, where the ICC has a long tradition of devising rules to help business in its international operations, and its Commission on Marketing and Advertising is the principal body for strategy building. This kind of self-regulation defines uniform standards in handling communication to consumers, which are adopted in areas where there are no agreed rules between the states, and which according to the ICC gain wide currency: "Because its member companies and associations are themselves engaged in international business, ICC has unrivalled authority in making rules that govern the conduct of business across borders. Although these rules are voluntary, they are observed in countless thousands of transactions every day and have become part of the fabric of international trade."[23]

Some pieces of self-regulation have had a long history. The ICC Code on Advertising Practice was issued in 1937, and has undergone several revisions, most recently in 2006 as the Consolidated ICC Code on Advertising and Marketing Communications Practice. Linked to this is the more specific ICC International Code of Direct Selling, adopted in 1978 and updated in 2007. Of further relevance for regulating the provision of information to consumers is the ICC/World Association for Social, Opinion and Market Research (ESOMAR) International Code on Market and Social Research, which dates back to 1948 and was last amended in 2007. These examples indicate that the ICC has a strong tradition in self-regulation that is relevant for large parts of global business, and that efforts are continuously invested in monitoring development and revising the codes. Here one important factor is the developments in digital media, as consumers are approached through new media and in new ways. Special attention is also needed to handle communication with new and expanding segments of consumers, such as young people, who in the past were not identified as an important and vulnerable group requiring special protection, and relevant guidelines can be found in the Compendium of ICC Rules on Children and Young People and Marketing. This is an area where the ICC has been a catalyst for action in specific industries, an issue we return to later, and some activities are managed by the broader initiative Business Action for Responsible Marketing and Advertising (BARMA).[24]

The ICC is, without comparison, the leading business association in global consumer policy, but there are other general organizations in business that are involved in certain aspects of consumer protection, but are not backed by the same historical legacy, and have the power to issue rules and foster compliance in business. While the ICC exchanges with several intergovernmental agencies, the pattern is different for the Business and Industry Advisory Committee to the OECD (BIAC) which, at its inception in 1962, was designed primarily to interact with the OECD and engage in policies, including consumer protection, that are embraced by the OECD itself. One can say that BIAC in many respects is committed to the same fields, not least because the OECD needs substantial input from business in adopting strategies and issuing various kinds of guidelines and recommendations, and BIAC seeks to have the same coverage as the OECD, namely representing business interests from the same countries and continents. This implies that BIAC attends to a number of issues in consumer protection that have been tabled for recent decades, such as the internet, conflict resolution, product safety and all the related documents adopted by the OECD.[25]

In recent years, financial consumer protection has also come to play a significant role, and this activity is relevant both to the financial industry as a specific segment of business, and to business in general because financial transactions relate to the entire business community. As with the ICC, the activities of BIAC are not just addressed under the label of competition policy, but are actively taken up as consumer protection proper. Coordination is required between the ICC and BIAC, but a major feature in the division of labor is simply institutional – they exchange with different international agencies.

This feature – the institutional link-up with selected intergovernmental entities – is further typical of the B20 Coalition (sometimes just referred to as B20), the platform of associations from the major economies preparing business strategies and participation in the wings of the Group of Twenty (G20) meetings.[26] The coalition is designed with the explicit purpose of working in this institutional context, and therefore labor is shared with both the ICC and the BIAC, which deliver input to the B20 Coalition to form a consolidated business voice. The coalition does not have strong secretariats like ICC and BIAC, but consults with these organizations or other actors to develop policies, including consumer issues, when necessary. A variety of policy-oriented task forces under the coalition draw on expertise among associations and corporations.

Although these summits are usually associated with the meetings between heads of states from the member countries, there are many other important and parallel activities; in this context, business coordinates and speaks with one voice where possible, and provides recommendations for G20 action. Given the encompassing and shifting agendas of these meetings, and the comparatively weak institutionalization of consumer policy at the global level, it is no surprise that consumer protection is rarely foregrounded and that meetings are packed with many other issues in global politics. Consumer affairs are often addressed in more indirect ways, for instance as an aspect of competition and trade policy, or within more specific issues such as anti-corruption, intellectual property rights or green growth. However, the financial crisis has led to a much greater focus on the financial sector and on how best to educate consumers in these markets. The G20 has been active in new initiatives to enhance financial consumer protection and, based on consensus in the business community, the B20 Coalition has delivered input into this process as well.[27]

While the ICC, BIAC and B20 Coalition coordinate and represent the interest of national business associations in consumer policy and many other areas, organizations such as the World Economic Forum (WEF) and the World Business Council for Sustainable Development (WBCSD) organize single corporations, most, if not all, being multinational and having a strong bias toward the affluent countries. Hence they cannot speak for business in the same representative manner. Both organizations, however, have a broad constituency because they cover several industries, although the WBCSD has firms with some kind of environmental profile as members. Their style is different from that of the ICC, BIAC and B20 Coalition, which have a different status in the international agencies with which they exchange, but gradually the WEF and WBCSD have established relations with some of the agencies, WBCSD primarily in the environmental field.[28] However, the two organizations do not tend to formulate concrete recommendations for governments and international agencies to adopt and implement in the same way as the ICC, BIAC and B20 Coalition. The WEF is a very influential actor and invests many resources in diagnosing problems, setting agendas and framing debates,[29] and to some degree this style also characterizes WBCSD, but it also focuses on concrete projects in selected industries. Their engagement in consumer protection is mainly indirect because the conditions of consumers are affected by many different policies and not labelled just as strategies toward consumers, but in some cases consumer protection is approached in a manifest way.

The WEF especially is involved in a vast number of issues and plays an important role in global agenda-setting in business and beyond, and it would be strange had the WEF not taken some initiatives in the field. The WEF has addressed the situation of consumers in relation to the internet, intellectual property rights and financial services, but stronger efforts appear to have been made with regard to sustainable production and consumption, and the organization encourages corporations toward responsible behavior in order to foster innovation and offer consumers better opportunities for making sustainable choices.[30] Of course, this is also a core activity of WBCSD,[31] which is engaged in a variety of projects on sustainable development in which sustainable consumption is intrinsic, often in relation to specific industries and producers. Many initiatives to address consumer protection, however, emerge outside the general organizations analyzed here and are advanced by the industries themselves and through industry associations and other initiatives.

Special business associations and related bodies engaged in consumer policy

While there are relatively few general associations and other broad initiatives embracing consumer policy from a business perspective, there is a large and differentiated group of industry associations and other entities attending to consumer protection within specific issues. In research, many approaches have developed to analyze self-regulation within industries and product groups, and they point to potentials as well as pitfalls of such arrangements. In some areas special business associations enjoy a privileged position and have very close collaboration with the designated international agencies. This is the case in some of the areas analyzed in the previous chapters. The food industry has strong relations with FAO; the pharmaceutical industry enjoys a solid position in its cooperation with the WHO; and the association of airline companies is an indispensable partner with ICAO. In these areas, consumer policy is relatively well developed and the agencies can draw on important knowledge and support – but sometimes also opposition – from the industries concerned. The relevant associations are not only capable of taking independent initiatives and providing qualified responses to the agencies, but in areas of consumer protection they also establish their own rule-systems to guide firms in their relations with consumers. Let us look at the three industries in turn.

At the global level, the pharmaceutical industry is organized through the International Federation of Pharmaceutical Manufacturers & Associations (IFPMA), which has official relations with the WHO. Relations with patients rank high on its agenda and therefore it can make important contributions to this field. One important activity, in addition to participation in many WHO processes, is the management of an industry code regulating the marketing of medicines.

In 1981 the organization adopted the IFPMA Code of Pharmaceutical Marketing Practices, not entirely without criticism from outside the industry, and it has been amended many times, the most recent revision being in 2012.[32] Patient safety and the provision of correct information are central elements in the code, and recent revisions have incorporated reference to more stakeholder groups, such as patient organizations, and new dimensions of communication, as well as changes in the various complaint procedures stipulated in the code. Although further progress can be made, the code plays a very important role in consumer protection and, interestingly enough, is not a voluntary code like so many other industry codes. Members – single corporations as well as national associations – must comply, otherwise sanctions may be imposed to make recalcitrant members abide by the rules and change their behavior. It must be emphasized that many national codes exist that establish national rules, but the IFPMA code guarantees standards for the activity of the industry in all countries, and therefore comes close to what might be adopted in the framework of intergovernmental organizations.

The situation in the food industry has some similarities with pharma, yet there are differences in the contribution of business to consumer policy. A chief factor is that the organization of the global food industry is not as centralized as pharmaceuticals, and instead we find a number of specialized organizations representing specific product groups within the broader food industry. It is also less globalized, with national and regional associations, for instance in the USA and Europe, not having the additional global superstructure needed to unite different interests, suggesting that exchanges with international agencies are often through a more fragmented organizational system of business associations. This is strongly reflected in the pattern of non-governmental organizations awarded different forms of consultative status with FAO: there are a number of associations from the food industry but no single voice.[33] However, in some areas global collective action is accomplished, an example being the International Food and Beverage Alliance (IFBA), which is more focused on the WHO and its work than on FAO. This institutional orientation is taken because nutrition is a field that crosses both food policy and health policy.

The alliance started life in 2008 and today has a program of commitments on healthy lifestyles which is a follow-up to the WHO Global Strategy on Diet, Physical Activity and Health endorsed in 2004. The IFBA has therefore been challenged to formulate strategies to combat obesity and advance healthy lifestyles by defining rules for nutrition information for consumers and for advertising and marketing to children, for which the Global Policy on Advertising and Marketing Communications to Children has been adopted as one of several global policies.[34] The ICC Framework for Responsible Food and Beverage Market Communication has been an inspiration here. The IFBA invests much energy in administering self-regulation, which is formulated through so-called global policies, but it can be questioned how strict these commitments in the food industry are.[35]

If we turn to air traffic and air passengers as a specific group of consumers, we find another pattern that is more similar to the position of the pharma industry. The airline companies have a very strong association that has always had a close collaboration with ICAO, the designated UN agency. Formed in 1945 but tracing its roots back to 1919, the International Aviation Transport Association (IATA) is the sole representative of the companies and, holding unique knowledge on many regulatory and technical issues, is intimately involved in much of ICAO's work. The IATA is keenly interested in "seeking a united government and industry approach to passenger rights that works for a global business and strikes a balance between ensuring adequate consumer protection and overburdening the industry and its customers with the costs of excessive regulatory compliance."[36] This is one of the many goals outlined in the Resolution on IATA Core Principles on Consumer Protection in 2013, which builds on its previously adopted Global Customer Service Framework.

The organization has further endorsed various commitments and best practices on behalf of the airlines, and these can be further improved through the strategies of single airline companies, which establish different profiles in competition. These efforts refer to conditions before, during and after the flight, such as various interline standards relating to passengers and baggage, and they go beyond what is defined in public regulation.[37] Many practices are geared to the interests of the airlines, of course, but are focused on the conditions of passengers, as for instance the Simplifying the Business (StB) initiative which, among other things, aims at getting passengers through the procedures at airports more quickly.[38]

On top of that, IATA has adopted programs to enhance passenger safety, a classical issue in air transport and today embraced by its Six-Point Safety Strategy. The industry initiatives include auditing, and are expressed through the IATA Safety Operational Audit (IOSA) and the IATA Safety Audit for Ground Operations (ISAGO). They exist in addition to conventions and other rules adopted in the framework of ICAO, but they have a broader perspective than consumer protection.

Related to air transport but having its own policy field is tourism, and here several private organizations in the industry formulate policies and exchange with the World Tourism Organization (UNWTO). The UNWTO receives input from many groups in tourism and many actors have joined the organization as affiliated members; they represent a mixed bag of interests, and are also involved in the policy processes leading to the adoption of UNWTO strategies. Tourism policy has some rules on consumer protection, as analyzed in Chapter 4, but compared with other agencies, measures are not impressive.

The industry is quite fragmented in terms of representation. It has been difficult to engage in joint action, and not all parts of the industry relate directly to end consumers. An important player is the World Travel & Tourism Council (WTTC), founded in 1990, which does not have policies that are directed primarily at consumers, although it is involved in the Hotel Carbon Measurement Initiative (HCMI), which may provide signals to certain consumer segments.

The World Travel Agents Associations Alliance (WTAAA), formed in 2005, represents business interests and "in addition to air transport policy, the WTAAA is expected to have input into a wide range of travel and tourism related issues including areas such as international cruise line and hotel policy."[39] Again, these policies have relevance for consumers but no explicit consumer strategy is adopted. We must therefore turn to other actors in the tourism industry to find organizations engaged in issues that appeal to consumers. Here important initiatives include the Code of Conduct for the Protection of Children from Sexual Exploitation in Travel and Tourism which is administered by an independent organization,[40] joined by leading tourism companies and backed by UNICEF and UNWTO; and the Global Sustainable Tourism Council (GSTC), which sets international standards for sustainable corporate behavior and provides the basis for the certification of companies and products.[41]

These examples indicate that interesting developments by business to address consumer protection often take place outside the framework of traditional and established business associations. There are many ways of creating and running these initiatives, and we now turn to arrangements managed by a variety of other actors in business often with parties outside business and addressing further issues of consumer protection.[42] It is typical of these initiatives that they have multiple ambitions and combine consumer concerns with a number of other goals, and that they tend to involve different interested parties to make arrangements that are legitimate and effective at the same time. We cannot do justice to this increasing complexity and the list (Table 5.3) is not exhaustive, but among the myriad of cases we characterize major examples from different industries and present them in the order discussed in this chapter.

As illustrated in Table 5.3, self-regulation exists in many sectors, from basic foods to luxury goods. They all relate to business because industries or single firms are supposed to join them, and in many cases business is a very active force behind their emergence and administration, thus they are different from the Global Compact and the ISO, dealt with in previous chapters. However, there are also cases in which independent parties outside the business community are major contributors or even the leading force, sometimes forming "multi-stakeholder arrangements" in which multiple actors and concerns are integrated to regulate a product or an industry.[43] In fact, today there is such a diversity of organizations that the conceptual language needed to categorize and analyze them is equally bewildering.

In many cases, private organizations administer a scheme that, in principle, could be managed by an intergovernmental body, but flexibility is sometimes greater outside this public framework. An important example is ICANN, established in 1998 to regulate the internet.[44] As briefly discussed in Chapter 4, this is an organization with many tasks, consumer protection being one of them, but the organization is complex and has its own unique setup. What is typically missing in these arrangements is the formal participation of traditional consumer organizations. CI, as the most prominent of all organizations in the global consumer movement, does not take part in these processes. This does not suggest that consumers are entirely missing, but consumer interests are represented in other ways.

There is no single model for all forms of private regulation. Yet some approaches are found in several sectors. The International Social and Environmental Accreditation and Labeling Alliance (ISEAL Alliance) was established in 2002 and makes available a standard-setting code, an impact code, and an assurance code for other organizations

Table 5.3 Examples of global self-regulation and consumer protection in different sectors

Industry and product	Organization
Advertising	International Chamber of Commerce; Business Action for Responsible Marketing and Advertising; International Advertising Association; World Federation of Advertisers
Health	International Federation of Pharmaceutical Manufacturers & Associations (drugs)
Airlines	International Aviation Transport Association
Tourism	Global Sustainable Tourism Organization; The Code
Telecommunications	Internet Corporation for Assigned Names and Numbers (internet)
Food	Marine Stewardship Council (fish); Aquaculture Stewardship Council (farmed seafood); Fair Trade International (coffee, tea, fruit, rice etc.); International Food & Beverage Alliance (food and beverages); GLOBALG.A.P. (food)
Forest products	Forest Stewardship Council
Clothes	Global Organic Textile Standard; Clean Clothes Campaign
Automobiles	International Organization of Motor Vehicle Manufacturers; Global Fuel Economy Initiative
Diamonds	Kimberley Process Certification Scheme; World Diamond Council

and industries to adopt and implement in specific businesses, and several organizations administering their own codes have joined the alliance.[45] In their own way these bodies contribute to solving various economic, social and environmental problems. This applies, for instance, to the Forest Stewardship Council (FSC), Marine Stewardship Council (MSC) and Aquaculture Stewardship Council (ASC), which have attracted attention among the wider public and offer consumers information on sustainable consumption.[46]

Also Fairtrade International, established in 1997 as Fairtrade Labelling Organizations International (FLO, today just Fairtrade International), is a member of ISEAL. Together with the World Fair Trade Organization (WFTO), another private body, Fairtrade International defined the Charter of Fair Trade Principles in 2009, and today these general principles govern major areas of fair trade and help guide consumers in the market. Fairtrade International's own principles and standards are applied in many industries where companies are audited and certified by a related but independent entity, FLOCERT, according to specific instructions.[47] Certification takes particular account of the role of labor (workers' rights and child labor) in the production chain, and through the fairtrade mark important information on economic, social and environmental conditions is disseminated to consumers. The basic idea is to foster a kind of partnership between particular groups of producers and consumers, and fair trade principles have become successful in many areas, especially in food.

There are many other examples of self-regulation in food, and here links are not between consumer and labor rights issues, but emphasis is placed on other economic and social relations.[48] GLOBALG.A.P. is a certification system for global agricultural practices and, according to the organization, it is "the world's leading farm assurance program, translating consumer requirements into good agricultural practice."[49] These practices comprise safety, sustainability, and worker and animal conditions, and are included in a Code of Conduct which, together with other rules on procedures and standards, is important for the different accredited bodies in auditing and certifying products and producers. Consumer concerns are central to this project, but consumers are not directly represented in the various bodies running the organizations, whereas representatives of retailers and producers participate in the board, and this model is common in many schemes.

The private regulation of food has attracted much scholarly attention, but beyond food we find a rich diversity of other global organizations committed to self-regulation and, in one way or another, responding to consumer demands. In clothes and textiles we find standard-setting bodies that combine different policy strategies: The Global Organic Textile Standard (GOTS), formed in 2002, has a clear consumer dimension, but labor and sustainability concerns are also filtered into its program on organic fibres. The Clean Clothes Campaign (CCC) is more concerned with labor conditions in the garment and sportswear industry, and it has a model code to set standards and appeal to certain segments of consumers.[50] It has a more aggressive style, although boycotts are not a general tool in its activities.

We have already discussed self-regulation in the area of air transport, but it is important to note that a more mundane means of transport, cars, is also characterized by some degree of self-regulation. In the past there was a strong focus on the safety of cars, a basic consumer issue of course, but more recent developments can be found with regard to sustainability and energy-saving initiatives, such as the World-Wide

Fuel Charter of the International Organization of Motor Vehicle Manufacturers (OICA) and the Global Fuel Economy Initiative (GFEI), in which the FIA Foundation, related to the international organization of motor car users (FIA, Fédération Internationale de l'Automobile), is involved.[51] Again, such measures can be critically important in the competition between car manufacturers, but definitely also appeal to consumers.[52] In a transport-related industry such as tourism we find kindred issues, although sustainability is here applied to a variety of services. This is, for instance, reflected in the work of the Global Sustainable Tourism Organization (GSTO).

There is a great variety of private organizations that engage in some kind of self-regulation with the explicit goal of protecting the interests of consumers and helping them make informed choices. The products range from everyday consumer goods to luxury goods. To round off this brief discussion on self-regulation, it is interesting to note that even goods such as precious stones offered to a highly selective audience are regulated by special private bodies.

As part of the Kimberley Process Certification Scheme (KPCS), which regulates certain aspects of trade in rough diamonds and is meant to prevent trade in "blood diamonds," the World Diamond Council (WDC) administers a System of Warranties for diamonds. Accordingly, buyers and sellers of diamonds must guarantee to consumers that diamonds are "conflict-free" and come from countries affiliated with the KPCS. In cases of non-compliance, offending members will be expelled from the WDC. There are many economic and political goals involved in this process, and peace and development are crucial here, but also the consumer dimension is highlighted, and important information on the origin of diamonds is disseminated to consumers who can influence trade in diamonds. As in many other cases of self-regulation, however, the implementation of rules is complex and the forces of the market are difficult to harness.[53] Promises are often hard to keep.

Conclusion

An analysis of global consumer organizations is not complete without studying the contributions of the consumer movement and organized business. They form an integral part of a complex organizational system where they represent different interests, participate in various forums, and take on specific tasks assigned to them. In the same way as intergovernmental agencies shape important conditions for action, these private organizations also facilitate or impede initiatives taken by the agencies.

First, it is obvious that the landscape of organizations in the global consumer movement is not very diversified. There are relatively few associations with a full commitment in consumer policy, with CI being the indisputable lead organization, having the capacity to embrace a rich variety of issues, pursue the same basic strategies in relation to different industries, and participate in the work of many agencies. Few other organizations represent consumers in specific sectors, and there is a further group of small and oscillating initiatives that are difficult to record. To understand collective action among consumers, we must develop theories that see collective action as encouraged by intra-organizational drivers, because both national and international associations have tools to assist each other and further facilitate cooperation. We also must understand collective action as stimulated by inter-organizational factors because many agencies stimulate coordination in the global consumer movement.

Second, business participates in global consumer policy through a large number of associations, but there are some organizations, such as the ICC, that have a relatively broad engagement, although not comparable with that of CI. In this way there is a kind of hierarchy in the global business community. Many industry associations are very active in their own domain and can mobilize and contribute specialized knowledge to advance or hinder initiatives from international agencies and consumer groups. However, not all business associations are astute in consumer policy, and many concentrate on other issues. It is also important to emphasize that there are other actors in business that are not organized in an associational format, and these initiatives and alliances are not properly conceptualized and theorized.

Third, business is increasingly active in the development of private alternatives to public regulation, either alone or together with civil society groups or independent third parties. Such forms of regulation proliferate at the global level and many of them address consumer concerns, often combined with other goals such as sustainability and human rights. Examples of self-regulation cut across the business community, while others pertain to specific industries and products. Self-regulation has various pitfalls because its primary goal is not necessarily to work for the betterment of consumers, but to advance business interests. However, some forms of self-regulation respond to and integrate consumer concerns, and self-regulation is often a matter of aligning different goals. Further theoretical scrutiny of these private initiatives in consumer protection is required.

They have the potential to improve consumer protection, but in most cases there is no proper consumer participation in the bodies running self-regulation, and organizations are not always effective. However, the experiments with these forms of regulation show that there is much innovation in global consumer policy, and that we should constantly be aware of the new types of activities and relations that emerge and that today characterize the work of global consumer organizations.

Notes

1 For a broader discussion on the disadvantages of these big groups, Jonathan G.S. Koppell, *World Rule: Accountability, Legitimacy, and the Design of Global Governance* (Chicago, Ill.: University of Chicago Press, 2010), 230–64.

2 Gunnar Trumbull, *Strength in Numbers. The Political Power of Weak Interests* (Cambridge, Mass.: Harvard University Press, 2012).

3 In this context we do not include organizations with tasks such as product testing where, for instance, International Consumer Research & Testing (ICRT) is active. We have very little research on the global consumer movement. Studies on civil society organizations, social movements and advocacy groups largely ignore consumer organizations and few contributions discuss the role of CI. Karsten Ronit, "Modes of consumer participation and engagement in the making of global consumer policy," in *Global Public Policy: Business and the Countervailing Powers of Civil Society*, ed. Karsten Ronit (London: Routledge, 2007), 65–88; Matthew Hilton, *Prosperity for All: Consumer Activism in an Era of Globalization* (Ithaca, NY: Cornell University Press, 2009).

4 Consumers International, *About Us*, www.consumersinternational.org/who-we-are/about-us.

5 Ibid.

6 This is reflected in research on institutions, capacity building, social capital and political order. One of the key works has been Francis Fukuyama, *State-Building: Governance and World Order in the Twenty-First Century* (Ithaca, NY: Cornell University Press, 2004), a book that has generated much debate. Consumers International is assisted by international agencies, for instance ISO, to encourage the participation of domestic consumer organizations and, eventually, help them improve the input of their governments into international agencies, www.iso.org/iso/prodsservices/otherp ubs/pdf/copolcobrochure_2005-en.pdf.

7 This model of organizing interests was originally theorized in Robert H. Salisbury, "An exchange theory of interest groups," *Midwest Journal of Political Science* 13, no. 1 (1969): 1–32. In this perspective, leaders of interest groups have important roles as individual entrepreneurs, turning associations into firms. A similar type of model can be found in Aseem Prakash and Mary Kay Gugerty, eds, *Advocacy Organizations and Collective Action* (Cambridge: Cambridge University Press, 2010).

8 CI launches campaigns, but its strategy is not to engage in boycotts. Boycotts are typically run by other actors, either by permanent organizations or by *ad hoc* initiatives, and often outside the traditional consumer movement. For an overview see Ethical Consumer, *Successful Boycotts – 1986 to 2009*, www.ethicalconsumer.org/portals/0/downloads/successful%20boycotts.pdf.

9 Attention to financial services is recent, and has been updated in the past decade. Consumers International, *Safe, Fair and Competitive Markets in Financial Services: Recommendations for the G20 on the Enhancement of Consumer Protection in Financial Services* (London: Consumers International, 2011), www.consumersinternational.org/media/669348/cifinancialrep ort2011.pdf.

10 Thomas G. Weisss and Leon Gordenker, eds, *NGOs, the UN, & Global Governance* (Boulder, Colo.: Lynne Rienner, 1996); Peter Willetts, *Non-Governmental Organizations in World Politics: The Construction of Global Governance* (Routledge: London, 2011); Karsten Ronit and Volker Schneider, eds, *Private Organizations in Global Politics* (London: Routledge, 2000).

11 Sometimes participation is seen in terms of "access": Jonas Tallberg, Thomas Sommerer, Theresa Squatrito and Christer Jönsson, *The Opening Up of International Organizations: Transnational Access in Global Governance* (Cambridge: Cambridge University Press, 2013). This may be useful to capture certain aspects of participation. It is important to remember, however, that non-governmental organizations are in some cases highly integrated and do not need to struggle for recognition, and that exchanges may include cases where non-governmental organizations take control of agencies and capture policies.

12 There are different sources on the participation of CI in permanent intergovernmental organizations, but the most authoritative is data provided by CI itself, www.consumersinternational.org/our-members/join-us!/accredita tion. A few others are also relevant, see http://ngo-db.unesco.org/r/or/en/ 1100020545. Consumers International maintains relations with a further group of bodies without being formally accredited, for instance the FSB and G20.

13 Francesca Bignami and Steve Charnowitz, "Transatlantic civil society dialogue," in *Transatlantic Governance in the Global Economy*, eds Mark A. Pollack and Gregory C. Shaffer (Lanham, Md.: Rowman & Littlefield, 2001), 255–84.

14 CUTS, *What is CUTS*, www.cuts-international.org/index.htm.

15 However, some of its affiliates seem to play a larger role in certain areas of coordination. Thus CUTS is very much involved in the work of the International Network of Civil Society Organisations on Competition (INCSOC): see http://incsoc.net/index.htm and http://incsoc.net/pdf/mem bers1_INCSOC.pdf.

16 The International Baby Food Action Network (IBFAN) is such an example. Consumers International was important in creating this initiative as well as the Pesticide Action Network (PAN); Mathew Hilton, "The death of a consumer society," *Transactions of the Royal Historical Society* (18) 2008: 211–36.

17 Center for Science in the Public Interest, *Codex Alimentarius Commission*, http://cspinet.org/International/main.htm#iacfo.

18 In many ways IAPA is a firm that offers certain services to customers. It has also been described as an *Unternehmung* (company): Niels Klussmann and Arnim Malik, *Lexikon der Luftfahrt*, 3rd edn (Heidelberg: Springer, 2012), 133.

19 Several business associations participate but no consumer organizations are involved, although in a bizarre way the Air Crash Victims Families Group

(ACVFG) could be listed as a kind of passenger organization. ICAO, 38th Session of the ICAO Assembly, 24 September to 4 October 2013, Montréal, *List of Delegates No. 10.0* (Montreal: International Civil Aviation Organization, 2013), 53.

20 Karsten Ronit, "Global business associations, self-regulation and consumer policy," in *Business and Sustainability: Between Government Pressure and Self-Regulation*, eds Achim Lang and Hannah Murphy (Heidelberg: Springer, 2014), 61–79.

21 Few studies give full attention to the ICC. Dominic Kelly, "The International Chamber of Commerce," *New Political Economy*, 10, no. 2 (2005): 259–71.

22 IATA has been characterized as "perhaps the most lavishly staffed international business organization in the world," John Braithwaite and Peter Drahos, *Global Business Regulation* (Cambridge: Cambridge University Press, 2000), 461.

23 ICC, *Advocacy, Codes and Rules.* www.iccwbo.org/advocacy-codes-and-rules.

24 Other global business associations have a long history of self-regulation in advertising. This applies, for instance, to the International Advertising Association (IAA), established in 1938, and the World Federation of Advertisers (WFA), established in 1953. Self-regulation of the advertising industry has repercussions for broader sections of business.

25 These issues are managed today by a special consumer policy group in BIAC, http://biac.org/policy_groups/consumer-policy.

26 Peter I. Hajnal, *The G8 System and the G20. Evolution, Role and Documentation* (Aldershot: Ashgate, 2007); John J. Kirton, *G20 Governance for a Globalized World* (Aldershot: Ashgate, 2013); Andrew F. Cooper and Ramesh Thakur, *The Group of Twenty (G20)* (London: Routledge, 2013).

27 ICC/G20 Advisory Group, *G20 Business Scorecard*, 2nd edn (Paris: International Chamber of Commerce, 2013), 32.

28 There are other organizations with some relevance for consumers, but they are basically created to defend business interests. The International Anti-Counterfeiting Coalition (IACC) is such an example, but it is a US initiative with international duties rather than an international organization. Re-Act: The Anti-Counterfeiting Network, however, is based in Europe but is increasingly globalizing.

29 Geoffrey Allen Pigman, *The World Economic Forum. A Multi-Stakeholder Approach to Global Governance* (London: Routledge, 2006).

30 Some reports have been published by the WEF's Consumer Industry Agenda Council, for instance *Sustainability for Tomorrow's Consumer The Business Case for Sustainability* (Geneva: World Economic Forum, 2009); *Consumer Industry Emerging Trends and Issues* (Geneva: World Economic Forum, 2011); *Engaging Tomorrow's Consumer* (Geneva: World Economic Forum, 2014).

31 WBCSD, *Sustainable Production and Consumption. A Business Perspective* (Geneva: World Business Council for Sustainable Development, 1996); WBCSD, *A Vision for Sustainable Consumption* (Geneva: World Business Council for Sustainable Development, 2011). ICC is also active in sustainability and sees sustainability in terms of customer relations: ICC, *The Business Charter for Sustainable Development* (Paris: International

Chamber of Commerce, 2000); ICC, *Framework for Environmental Marketing Communication* (Paris: International Chamber of Commerce, 2011).

32 IFPMA, *IFPMA Code of Practice 2012* (Geneva: International Federation of Pharmaceutical Manufacturers & Associations, 2012).

33 FAO, *INGOs with Formal Status* (Rome: FAO, 2013), www.fao.org/fileadm in/user_upload/partnerships/docs/2013%20INGOs%20with%20formal%20sta tus.pdf.

34 IFBA, *Global Policy on Advertising and Marketing Communications to Children*, November 2011. In addition, we find the *IFBA Principles for a Global Approach to Fact-based Nutrition Labeling*, November 2010, and the *IFBA Global Policy on Marketing Communications to Children* and the *IFBA Principles for a Global Approach to Fact-based Nutrition Information*, both revised September 2014.

35 Corinna Hawkes and Jennifer L. Harris, "An analysis of the content of food industry pledges on marketing to children," *Public Health Nutrition* 14, no. 8 (2011): 1403–14.

36 IATA, *Resolution on IATA Core Principles on Consumer Protection*. Press Release No. 32, 3 June 2013.

37 ICAO, *Summary of Consumer Protection Rules* (Montreal: International Civil Aviation Organization, 2013). See www.icao.int/sustainability/Docum ents/ConsumerProtection_Table-A.pdf.

38 This program was launched in 2004. IATA, *Simplifying the Business Leading Transformation for Customer-Centric Air Travel* (Montreal: International Civil Aviation Organization, 2014).

39 World Travel Agents Association Alliance, *Press Release*, April 20, 2005.

40 Thecode.org, *The Code of Conduct for the Protection of Children from Sexual Exploitation in Travel and Tourism*, www.thecode.org/about/history; GSTC, *Creating Universal Principles*, www.gstcouncil.org/gstc-criteria/susta inable-tourism-gstc-criteria.html. Such initiatives are best studied from an institutionalist perspective. C. Michael Hall, "Framing behavioral approaches to understanding and governing sustainable tourism consumption: beyond neoliberalism, 'nudging' and 'green growth?'" *Journal of Sustainable Tourism* 21, no. 7 (2013): 1091–109.

41 Business behavior typically includes a consumer component. David Vogel, *The Market for Virtue. The Potential and Limits of Corporate Social Responsibility* (Washington, DC: Brookings Institution Press, 2005). Business independently takes consumer concerns into consideration, and sometimes consumers are involved in a dialogue and invited into a formal arrangement.

42 Luc W. Fransen and Ans Kolk, "Global rule-setting for business: a critical analysis of multi-stakeholder standards," *Organization* 14, no. 5 (2007): 667–84.

43 For some of these developments related to civil society, see Milton L. Mueller, *Networks and States: The Global Politics of Internet Governance* (Boston, Mass.: MIT Press, 2010).

44 International Social and Environmental Accreditation and Labeling Alliance, *Full Members*, www.isealalliance.org/our-members/full-members.

45 Especially forestry has been researched. For an analysis of the early years, see Benjamin Cashore, Graeme Auld and Deanna Newsome, *Governing through Markets. Forest Certification and the Emergence of Non-State*

Authority (New Haven, Conn.: Yale University Press, 2004). Today the credibility of the FSC is questioned by watchdogs such as FSC-Watch.

46 Fairtrade International Standards and related information available online, www.fairtrade.net/fileadmin/user_upload/content/2009/standards/docum ents/2014-05-15_List_of_Fairtrade_Standards.pdf. Gavin Fridell, *Fair Trade Coffee: The Prospects and Pitfalls of Market-Driven Social Justice* (Toronto: Toronto University Press, 2007).

47 Jennifer Clapp and Doris Fuchs, eds, *Corporate Power in Global Agrifood Governance* (Boston, Mass.: MIT Press, 2009); Axel Marx, Miet Maertens, Johan Swinnen and Jan Wouters, eds, *Private Standards and Global Governance. Economic, Legal and Political Perspectives* (Cheltenham: Edward Elgar, 2012).

48 GLOBALG.A.P. *History*, www.globalgap.org/uk_en/who-we-are/about-us/history.

49 Business behavior and consumer behavior are linked in many ways. M.L. Loureiro and J. Lotade, "Do fair trade and eco-labels in coffee wake up the consumer conscience?," *Ecological Economics* 53 (2005): 129–38; Brenden E. Kendall, Rebecca Gill and George Cheney, "Consumer activism and corporate social responsibility. How strong a connection?," in *The Debate over Corporate Social Responsibility*, eds Steve May, George Cheney and Juliet Roper (Oxford: Oxford University Press, 2007), 242–64.

50 Tony Porter, "Climate change, private voluntary programs and the automobile industry," in *Business and Climate Policy: The Potentials and Pitfalls of Private Voluntary Programs*, ed. Karsten Ronit (Tokyo: United Nations University Press, 2012).

51 Competition between "leaders" and "laggards" is a classical issue in self-regulation. See Neil Gunningham, Robert A. Kagan and Dorothy Thornton, *Shades of Green: Business, Regulation, and Environment* (Stanford, Calif.: Stanford University Press, 2003).

52 For a critical assessment of self-regulation, see David Vogel, "The private regulation of global corporate conduct. Achievements and limitations," *Business & Society* 49, no. 1 (2010): 68–87.

6 Conclusion

- **Historical pathways**
- **Self-directed actors**
- **Knowledge bases**
- **Policy transfers**
- **Getting, defending and conquering new turf**
- **Collective action among consumers and in business**
- **State, market and civil society**

This chapter brings together the key findings of the book and elucidates the patterns of activity found in global consumer organizations – following the broad definition of these actors in the introduction. Although global consumer policy and global consumer organizations still may seem ill-defined, we have now a better understanding of how these patterns have emerged, how this complex field is actually organized, what kinds of actors are involved, and what kinds of activities they are engaged in.

After we briefly discuss how international agencies, the consumer movement and the corporate world are structured and contribute to the development of this area of politics, and then return to the basic questions raised in the introduction, we ask how the experiences from this policy field can inform the analysis of global institutions – the public and the private – more generally. Many of the findings can be used to address issues that currently pose a challenge to research on global institutions.

As to the general pattern of international agencies, there is a bewildering variety of organizations, committees and working groups available to manage consumer policy in all its different facets. There are, however, also forces trying to define broader strategies and principles for consumer protection as a whole and thereby overcome fragmentation, but usually these entities cover a smaller policy field – whether it be the general, the special, or the coordinating bodies. Very few initiatives seek to embrace consumer policy on a broader basis and play a directing role, and we can find many dynamics and bottom-up activities.

Consumer groups are confronted with serious challenges in the organization of interests and in the formulation of strategies for people whose basic conditions are so different. Nevertheless, and somewhat astonishingly, consumers have managed to organize interests in a coherent format. Consumers are active in many fields, although it is difficult to establish and maintain the required knowledge, but consumers are consulted by and welcomed into many intergovernmental organizations, although participation varies significantly. It is an important feature of most consumer organizations that they give high priority to public regulation and are critical of alternative forms of regulation proposed by some parts of the business community.

Business is represented in global consumer policy through a rich diversity of actors. Although there is much fragmentation, we also find organizations speaking for large parts of the global business community, and seeking to formulate general strategies, sometimes with a view to addressing issues from the perspective of competition policy. Business associations participate actively in the work of international agencies, but with substantial variation, and in many cases they have a preference for rules adopted in international agencies, while being critical of other elements of consumer protection. At the same time, business is an advocate of some forms of self-regulation, a dynamic but fragmented field of rule-making.

These brief answers will be expanded on when we discuss the findings in a more theoretical light, and the theoretical perspectives will give us some further clues as to the role of the different types of organizations. We begin here with the historical processes.

Historical pathways

Global consumer policy is not a very old and established policy field, and there is no single organization that defines and defends traditions. Yet the policy field has evolved over many decades, and gradually consumer issues have found their way into many organizations. Major parts of this development are characterized by evolution: small, sometimes very small, steps have brought consumer issues onto the agenda of international agencies. This evolutionary perspective is used to study changes in domestic politics but is also highly relevant when examining certain areas of global politics, in our case consumer policy.[1]

Sometimes small changes have affected greater transformations and led to the adoption of encompassing strategies and rules enhancing consumer protection, but initiatives to improve consumer protection have often been stalled. In the 1970s and 1980s there was definitely a momentum in consumer protection, but also in efforts to halt and moderate advances. The smaller steps and lack of progress can be explained by the sometimes discrete, sometimes pervasive battles between business and consumers, a point we return to below.

This process of many small steps is influenced by institutional fragmentation. Initiatives tend to be generated by many different public and private sources that separately bring consumer concerns forward in many different forums, following no central plan. Organizations such as the OECD and UNCTAD, CI and ICC, seem in their unique ways capable of stimulating broad initiatives, but their reach is limited.

With intervals, we have witnessed some major leaps forward, the adoption and revision of the UN Guidelines for Consumer Protection being an important example, but also issues such as sustainable consumption, internet regulation and financial education, which in different areas enhance consumer protection and document accomplished or imminent changes. They are engendered by different material and ideational factors, such as the emergence of new technologies (internet), a greater awareness (sustainability) or a crisis in markets (finance), but other factors can be involved and need further scrutiny.

Self-directed actors

Intergovernmental organizations are manifestations of important international bureaucracies, but the bureaucracies in consumer policy are scattered among many different agencies. In many of the bodies reviewed in this book, we find various departments, committees and working groups designated to consumer affairs, but these usually play a minor role in the organizations, which have many other commitments. The permanent entities are tasked with focusing strong attention on consumer affairs on a global scale, and they provide a certain degree of continuity to the field. They develop their own understandings and perspectives, which cannot be derived simply from the states and their priorities, and in many ways they help states to formulate their strategies. In other words, intergovernmental organizations can in some respects be regarded as "self-directed actors."[2]

The sources of autonomy are manifold and can be analyzed from different theoretical approaches. Constructivist thinking would emphasize the unique norms and values characterizing entities that are occupied with improving consumer protection, while rational perspectives would rather highlight the self-interest of these bodies to evade control and define their own strategies. Although arguments differ, both sets of theories suggest that agencies cannot be minutely controlled by the states, and in addition, that states prefer to grant agencies some kind of autonomy in managing consumer policy.

We have seen that organizations generally have broad mandates and have unique capabilities to interpret these. A factor here is the supply of information from their members, and some organizations, such as the OECD, can draw on rich sources of knowledge from those states that already have rich experiences with regulation. Interestingly, this provides opportunities for strong and well founded initiatives by agencies, but it also gives certain member states opportunities to follow their work more closely. It seems that countries from the most affluent parts of the world are able to assist intergovernmental organizations to gain some kind of autonomy and, at the same time, have relevant experiences as well as institutions to control the same agencies. The situation for countries from the Global South is very different. Therefore we need to differentiate between member states if we want to analyze agencies as self-directed actors in consumer policy.

Knowledge bases

Some agencies formulate a mission statement pertaining to consumers, but more than a simple mission statement is needed when building appropriate policies. Knowledge is required to formulate strategies and adopt regulation to protect consumers. In addition to knowledge on consumer protection and the broader principles adopted, profound knowledge is needed in different areas such as trade policy and competition policy, and in comparatively narrow fields such as food safety and air traffic. Unlike the member states, intergovernmental bodies have unique global obligations: they receive and evaluate experiences from around the world, and their global knowledge base is therefore entirely different from those of their members.

In some of the literature, knowledge is considered a distinct asset that can boost the position of the agencies in relation to their members,[3] and this is relevant in consumer policy too, but we need to extend this perspective and see knowledge in a somewhat broader institutional context. In fact, agencies are not always capable of monopolizing some forms of knowledge, and not only because other agencies may be active in the same field. In the consumer movement and in business, as well as in many other types of global organizations, similar types of knowledge are often accumulated, and different private organizations even dispose of alternative sources of knowledge. This makes it possible for a range of private organizations to challenge the existing knowledge of intergovernmental bodies or, in other cases, to share information, combine knowledge and develop joint approaches.

In research, it has been argued that international epistemic communities are found in many policy fields.[4] These communities involve experts from different organizations who typically share the same professional background and outlook. This perspective is also valid here and can be applied to areas of consumer policy where efforts are made to define general principles of consumer protection, where activities are developed to address certain industries and segments of consumers, and where coordination involves several agencies. Over time, very close collaboration has evolved between particular agencies and consumers and business, and these actors share many experiences and have the same understanding of many issues, but there are also limits to this collaboration.

Policy transfers

Many intergovernmental organizations are active in shaping global consumer policy, but they take on different roles. While some organizations seem relatively isolated without any opportunity to influence the broader avenues of consumer protection, others have a prominent role and see this as one of their missions. However, only a few bodies are attributed such a status. Both the OECD and UNCTAD have their own separate commitments and they are very conscious about this. These organizations are actively involved in policy transfer, but this is not a one-sided process where they seek to promote their ideas and experiences, because other organizations also seek and draw inspiration from these organizations. Studies on policy transfer and intergovernmental organizations have mainly analyzed how these agencies influence domestic policies in the broader context of globalization.[5] However, it is important to examine the relations between the different international agencies and recognize that there is a division of labor and a transfer of certain principles and strategies between them.

Their role in policy transfer comes from different sources. In consumer protection, the OECD represents countries having the most advanced models, and therefore has quite solid experiences to draw from. This implies, for instance, that some policy elements are transferred to UNCTAD. UNCTAD, for its part, is in a different position, but it currently has a lead role in the UN process of revising the UN guidelines. It is obvious, however, that this role is not fully manifested, because other organizations could to a higher degree draw on and refer to the UN Guidelines for Consumer Protection. Immersed in their own, often specialized agendas, many agencies only occasionally exploit some of the general ideas formulated in global consumer policy.

We cannot grasp the process of policy transfer fully if we study only the international agencies, and we therefore have to study policy transfer in an extended perspective. We must remember that both the consumer movement and organized business formulate strategies, which they communicate to the agencies, who very much need this kind of input. Private organizations dispose of important knowledge that is not always available in intergovernmental organizations, and they also represent important interests and thus possess an equally important source of legitimacy. Therefore the different private organizations are active in policy transfer, but they also assist the agencies in building up their strategies and transferring them to other actors at the global or national level.

Getting, defending and conquering new turf

Very few organizations are founded with the categorical and primary purpose of forwarding consumer protection, but over time a number of agencies have entered the field and added a variety of consumer issues to their policy portfolio. In the literature, such "territories" controlled by organizations have been referred to as "turf," and in the perspective of bureaucratic politics the process of getting, defending and conquering new turf is examined.[6]

The various turfs of the organizations are defined to avoid duplication, at least excessive overlaps, but in several cases we have witnessed that both some of the general and some of the special organizations are engaged in the same areas. This is perhaps most visible in cases when the organizations are asked to coordinate activities.

Although organizations with more or less identical tasks may bring forward different and even competing positions, certain overlaps can give a better understanding of neighboring organizations and their work. From the perspective of the member states, it can also be an advantage when there are some overlapping turfs, because several organizations will be available for a given job – and different states may prefer different organizations. This was vividly illustrated by the work on the regulation of MNCs in the 1970s and 1980s, an area in which UNCTAD invested much energy, but in which Western countries preferred action through the OECD to moderate or even avoid regulation. This is a kind of venue shifting that entails different opportunities for the member states.[7]

It is important to remember, however, that consumer policy is not always given high priority. For most of the organizations, their turf is clearly circumscribed and attending to consumer policy is a natural undertaking, but they are careful not to expand this activity too much. Indeed, the organizations typically have many missions, and consumer issues must compete for attention. Moreover, their strategies are not always formulated in terms of consumer policy but rather in the language of other, related policies. These factors moderate ambitions to engage in consumer policy and conquer new turf.

Collective action among consumers and in business

Consumers and firms face starkly different challenges in organizing collective action. While consumers are generally tied to local markets, although transactions have become more complex with the emergence of the internet, many firms, especially the very large corporations, are highly mobile, operate within large spaces and unfold trans-boundary activities – tellingly, the regulation of MNCs as a particularly influential group of corporations is a perennial goal for the consumer movement.

While business abounds with global associations, it seems a huge, almost impossible task to organize the dispersed consumers of the world. However, there are global organizations that may not organize consumers on an individual basis, but at least represent them, the paradigm case being CI. It can be disputed how representative these organizations really are, and how they contribute to global governance.[8] They draw members from the industrialized nations, a traditional area of associability, but perhaps most important of all, it is a question of whether they can legitimately speak for the impoverished masses in the developing countries. Size, but also legitimacy, are important dimensions of collective action.[9]

The existence of an all-encompassing association for consumers is somewhat counterintuitive. The standard version of collective-action theory teaches us that it is very hard or even impossible to achieve large-scale collective action, and that difficulty must definitely apply to this case. However, we have to analyze the peculiar historical background of the organizations for global consumers to enable us to understand what has made this kind of organization feasible. It must be remembered that the consumer movement has evolved quite unevenly around the world, with some of the pioneering countries taking a lead in the global organization of consumers. Organizations from a number of developed countries have played a major role in building a global movement, getting members for it and funding it, and assistance is provided where local consumer movements are weak or non-existent. If we proceed from analyzing these organizations in the consumer movement only from the perspective of the scale of collective action, then we neglect the different institutional factors that drive these organizations and make collective action possible.

State, market and civil society

A much debated issue in the current debate on global governance is the role played by state, market and civil society – signifying mechanisms of resource allocation that were considered important in the report from the Commission on Global Governance. Research on global governance has attributed different meanings to this concept,[10] but if we conceive of governance in the way outlined by the commission, we find different avenues for governing societies, and this applies to consumer affairs as well.

Approaches to intergovernmental organizations – whether seen as controlled by or gaining independence from states – cannot alone explain the development of global consumer policy. Affected interests on both the consumer and the business side have an important impact on the activities of these agencies. In many cases, participation in these various bodies is strongly encouraged and highly formalized, and in each their ways organized consumers and business contribute resources and strategies. Without these actors, agencies would not function effectively and legitimately but, as mentioned above, it is evident that these interested parties can block initiatives, which is also a way of demonstrating their impact.

In this study on global consumer organizations we have shown that state, market and civil society are all active as governance mechanisms, but their positions are quite uneven. In global consumer politics, the main role of civil society is to influence the behavior of firms in the market, and to leverage intergovernmental organizations to adopt policies beneficial to consumer protection in all its dimensions.

Thus civil society has a different status in the governance hierarchy: it does not have the capacity to establish an independent system of authority – except perhaps for ruling by way of moral standards. However, it is important to stress that some consumer groups are integrated into these other governance mechanisms when public regulation is adopted or when business self-regulation is established, and consumer groups can take an active role in setting agendas and devising strategies in these forums. In general, the consumer movement has a clear preference for public regulation of the market, but in some

industries actors outside the mainstream consumer movement contribute to and run various schemes of self-regulation. Thus consumer policy
has many forms, and this has consequences for our research strategy.

Global consumer organizations have gone largely unobserved in
research on international affairs, but this book shows that important
activities have unfolded to protect consumers, although efforts tend to
be fragmented, and therefore a flexible strategy is needed to capture
such a diverse phenomenon. It is also clear that there is much to gain
theoretically if we recognize that the organizations constitute a highly
complex group of actors, and that consumer policy is actually a diversity
of policies.

Notes

1 An analytical framework that emphasizes the evolutionary character of
change seems most relevant in the case of global consumer policy (see
James Mahoney and Kathleen Thelen, eds, *Explaining Institutional
Change. Ambiguity, Agency, and Power*, Cambridge: Cambridge University
Press, 2010), but it needs to be applied to the study of international organization and policy. This requires, for instance, that many institutional
layers and contextual factors be added to the evolutionary perspective, but
it is important that we also understand the changes in actors and how they
adapt to changing environments. This requires that the analysis can also be
nested at the level of actors; see John R. Alford and John R. Hibbing, "The
origin of politics: an evolutionary theory of political behavior," *Perspectives on
Politics* 2, no. 4 (2004): 707–23. Again, however, such actors need to be specified.
2 Under the concept of "self-directed actors," Joel E. Oestreich accom-
modates different theories that ascribe some kind of autonomy to intergovernmental organizations (IGOs): Joel E. Oestreich, *International
Organizations as Self-Directed Actors. A Framework for Analysis* (London:
Routledge, 2012). Ontologically different, rational and constructivist theories have offered a number of complementary answers to the role of IGOs
during the past decade: Michael N. Barnett and Martha Finnemore, *Rules
for the World. International Organizations and Global Politics* (Ithaca, NY:
Cornell University Press, 2004); Darren G. Hawkins, David A. Lake, Daniel
L. Nielson and Michael Tierney, eds, *Delegation and Agency in International
Organizations* (Cambridge: Cambridge University Press, 2006).
3 The possession of unique knowledge characterizes intergovernmental
organizations: Ernst B. Haas, *When Knowledge is Power. Three Models of
Change in International Organizations* (Los Angeles, Calif.: University of
California Press, 1990). The many cases of consumer organizations in this
book show that this knowledge includes both "scientific" and "consensual"
knowledge.
4 Mai'a K. Davis Cross, "Rethinking epistemic communities twenty years
later," *Review of International Studies*, 39, no. 1 (2013): 137–60.
5 Originally, policy transfer was mainly studied as the importation of policies
into the domestic arena, and here international organizations were

important in the transfer. David P. Dolowitz and David Marsh, "Learning from abroad: the role of policy transfer in contemporary policy-making," *Governance* 13, no. 1 (2000): 5–23. This perspective is relevant in consumer policy where developing countries seem to be the primary importers, because consumer policy and institutions have emerged elsewhere. It is necessary, however, to recognize the multiple roles that intergovernmental organizations can play; see Diane Stone, "Transfer and translation of policy," *Policy Studies* 33, no. 6 (2012): 483–99. As we have seen in this book, this includes the policy transfer between various international agencies in a given policy field, in which they hold different positions.

6   Maximizing budgets is a basic feature to enhance territories, and it is studied in research on bureaucratic politics: Anthony Downs, *Inside Bureaucracy* (New York: Harper and Row, 1957); William A. Niskanen, *Bureaucracy and Representative Government* (Chicago, Ill.: University of Chicago Press, 1971); James Q. Wilson, *Bureaucracy: What Government Agencies Do and Why They Do It* (New York: Basic Books, 1989). This perspective can also be applied to intergovernmental bodies, but in consumer policy only some organizations seem to take an active interest in task expansion. Some of the problems are studied as an aspect of inter-organizational coordination: Rafael Biermann, "Inter-organizational relations: an emerging research program," in *The Ashgate Research Companion to Non-State Actors*, ed. Bob Reinalda (Farnham: Ashgate, 2011): 173–84.

7   This option is discussed in principal-agent theory. See Darren G. Hawkins, David A. Lake, Daniel L. Nielson and Michael Tierney, "Delegation under anarchy: states, international organization, and principal-agent-theory," in *Delegation and Agency in International Organizations*, eds Darren G. Hawkins, David A. Lake, Daniel L. Nielson and Michael Tierney (Cambridge: Cambridge University Press, 2006), 3–38.

8   This problem is discussed with regard to "global democracy" by Daniele Archibugi, Mathias Koenig-Archibugi and Raffaele Marchetti, eds, *Global Democracy. Normative and Empirical Perspectives* (Cambridge: Cambridge University Press, 2012). Some studies focus more on the attributes of NGOs, for instance Peter A. Gourevitch, David A. Lake and Janice Gross Stein, eds, *The Credibility of Transnational NGOs. When Virtue is not Enough* (Cambridge: Cambridge University Press, 2012).

9   Gunnar Trumbull, *Strength in Numbers. The Political Power of Weak Interests* (Cambridge, Mass.: Harvard University Press, 2012).

10 Commission on Global Governance, *Our Global Neighborhood* (Oxford: Oxford University Press, 1995). It is important to bring together different forms of governance to arrive at a coherent analysis. However, it has always been difficult to find a place for civil society, often manifested through NGOs, in key theoretical approaches and study the roles of society, state and market in the global governance mix. See William Demars and Dennis Dijkzeul, eds, *The NGO Challenge for International Relations Theory* (London: Routledge, 2015). For a recent overview of the debate, see Thomas G. Weiss and Rorden Wilkinson, eds, *International Organization and Global Governance* (London: Routledge, 2014).

Select bibliography

Most research on consumer issues is done in the fields of economics, law and sociology, and to the extent that political science is involved, the focus is usually on domestic arrangements in consumer policy. In the area of international affairs in general and in international organization studies in particular, we find very few contributions. There is a stark difference between the significant scholarly interest in fields such as global environmental policy, global social policy or global health policy, and the modest concern for global consumer policy and its diverse and fragmented landscape of organizations. While we search largely in vain for contributions on global consumer policy and global consumer organizations, there are a number of books that examine national institutions and policies and that are available in English, but many other contributions are published in other languages. Consequently, the applicable literature in English is sparse; below are some examples of publications during the past fifteen years.

Stephen Brobeck and Robert N. Mayer, eds, *Watchdogs and Whistleblowers: A Reference Guide to Consumer Activism* (Santa Barbara, Calif.: ABC-CLIO, 2015). As the title suggests, this book covers many issues in consumer policy, and although it has a US bias, we find many entries on national and international actors which in one way or another are involved in consumer protection. Of course, many issues and actors are treated only briefly in this encyclopedia, but it is a good starting point and guide to other sources, and having been written by more than 100 specialists from around the world, it provides quick and concrete insights into many activities in consumer policy. This is a much updated and completely new version of similar encyclopedias published in 1991 and 1997.

Dietlind Stolle and Michele Micheletti, *Political Consumerism: Global Responsibility in Action* (Cambridge: Cambridge University Press, 2013). The authors offer an alternative approach to consumer affairs; they do not view these from the perspective of public policy and public regulation, but see the choices of consumers in the market as an instance of political activism and political participation. The approach is stronger in explaining consumer behavior than in explaining institution building. Emphasis is on developments in Western democracies.

David Vogel, *The Politics of Precaution: Regulating Health, Safety, and Environmental Risk in Europe and the United States* (Princeton, N.J.: Princeton University Press, 2012). This book complements a number of other earlier studies by David Vogel in the area of consumer policy and neighboring policy fields, and it shows that consumer interests are affected in different domains. The focus is international but not global, and the key emphasis is on describing and explaining the regulation in a comparative perspective.

Matthew Hilton, *Prosperity for All: Consumer Activism in an Era of Globalization* (Ithaca, NY and London: Cornell University Press, 2009). Written by a historian, this book takes a broad perspective on consumer issues and how they have developed in a historical context, especially after the Second World War. It not only covers the affluent countries where consumer protection is most advanced, but also includes a number of developing countries where consumer policy is unfolding. From the perspective of global consumer organizations, this book is also valuable in that it includes chapters on the international consumer movement and international consumer policy.

Gunnar Trumbull, *Consumer Capitalism: Politics, Product Markets, and Firm Strategy in France and Germany* (Ithaca, NY and London: Cornell University Press, 2006). Trumbull's treatise is written in the comparative politics tradition as a study of two major European countries. It identifies major areas of consumer protection, examines the different policies and processes, and explains how the countries have arrived at different models.

Even Lange and Iselin Theien, eds, *Affluence and Activism: Organised Consumers in the Post-War Era* (Oslo: Academic Press, 2004). This small book traces the development in a few Western countries (Britain, USA, France and Norway) and offers a comparative investigation into different consumer-policy models. These differences are important in evaluating the different domestic backgrounds for the formation of global consumer policy.

Matthew Hilton, *Consumerism in Twentieth-century Britain: The Search for a Historical Movement* (Cambridge: Cambridge University Press, 2003). Hilton examines different dimensions of consumerism in British society in a long-term perspective, and the investigation of consumer cultures and consumer ideologies is very much interwoven with the broader economic and social development of society. Although the book focuses mainly on domestic processes, certain international perspectives are included in the analysis as there are many link-ups with international efforts in economy, society and politics, particularly for later decades.

Patricia L. Maclachlan, *Consumer Politics in Postwar Japan: The Institutional Boundaries of Citizen Activism* (New York: Columbia University Press, 2002). This is another interesting book which concentrates on domestic process and the role played by the consumer movement, which adds important perspectives to a group of studies that are interested mainly in the conditions in Western countries.

Alasdair Young and Helen Wallace, *Regulatory Politics in the Enlarging European Union: Weighing Civic and Producer Interests* (Manchester: Manchester University Press, 2000). This volume analyses different sectors of the economy and explores how economic actors are regulated. Although the studies are not always framed in the language of consumer protection, it shows the basic conflicts between different concerns and how consumer policy is linked to competition policy.

Index

Routledge Global Institutions Series

6 Global Environmental Institutions (2006)
by Elizabeth R. DeSombre (Wellesley College)

5 Internal Displacement (2006)
Conceptualization and its consequences
by Thomas G. Weiss (The CUNY Graduate Center) and
David A. Korn

4 The UN General Assembly (2005)
by M. J. Peterson (University of Massachusetts, Amherst)

3 United Nations Global Conferences (2005)
by Michael G. Schechter (Michigan State University)

2 The UN Secretary-General and Secretariat (2005)
by Leon Gordenker (Princeton University)

1 The United Nations and Human Rights (2005)
A guide for a new era
by Julie A. Mertus (American University)

Books currently under contract include:

The Regional Development Banks
Lending with a regional flavor
by Jonathan R. Strand (University of Nevada)

Millennium Development Goals (MDGs)
For a people-centered development agenda?
by Sakiko Fukuda-Parr (The New School)

The Bank for International Settlements
The politics of global financial supervision in the age of high finance
by Kevin Ozgercin (SUNY College at Old Westbury)

International Migration
by Khalid Koser (Geneva Centre for Security Policy)

Human Development
by Richard Ponzio

The United Nations as a Knowledge Organization
by *Nanette Svenson (Tulane University)*

The International Criminal Court
The politics and practice of prosecuting atrocity crimes
by *Martin Mennecke (University of Copenhagen)*

BRICS
by *João Pontes Nogueira (Catholic University, Rio de Janeiro) and Monica Herz (Catholic University, Rio de Janeiro)*

Expert Knowledge in Global Trade
edited by *Erin Hannah (University of Western Ontario), James Scott (King's College London), and Silke Trommer (University of Helsinki)*

The European Union (2nd edition)
Clive Archer (Manchester Metropolitan University)

Protecting the Internally Displaced
Rhetoric and reality
Phil Orchard (University of Queensland)

The Arctic Council
Within the far north
Douglas C. Nord (Umea University)

For further information regarding the series, please contact:

Nicola Parkin, Editor, Politics & International Studies
Taylor & Francis
2 Park Square, Milton Park, Abingdon
Oxford OX14 4RN, UK
Nicola.parkin@tandf.co.uk
www.routledge.com

Printed in Great Britain
by Amazon